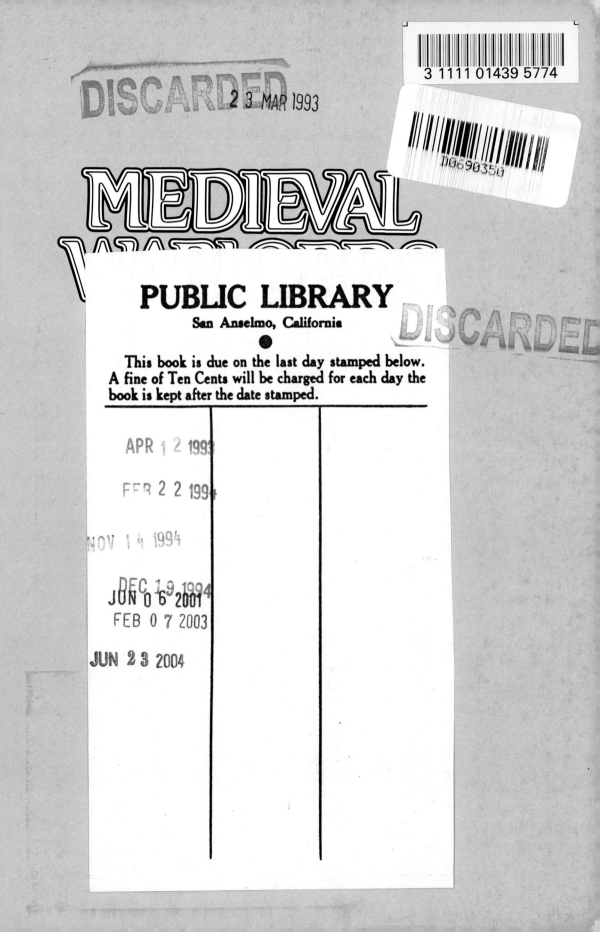

3 1111 01439 5774

ID0690350

MEDIEVAL WARLORDS

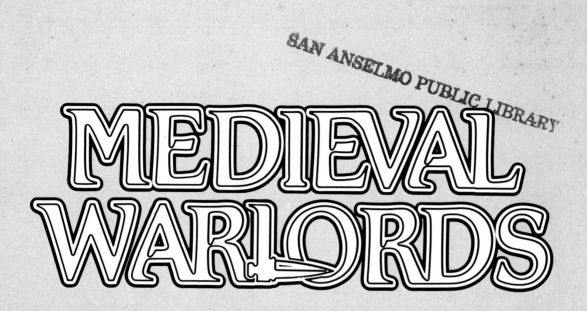

MEDIEVAL WARLORDS

TIM NEWARK

Colour illustrations by Angus McBride

BLANDFORD

For my father

Blandford
An imprint of Cassell
Villiers House, 41/47 Strand, London WC2N 5JE

First published 1987
This paperback edition published 1990
Reprinted 1991

Distributed in the United States by
Sterling Publishing Co. Inc.
387 Park Avenue South, New York, NY 10016-8810

Distributed in Australia by
Capricorn Link (Australia) Pty Ltd
PO Box 665, Lane Cove, NSW 2066

British Library Cataloguing in Publication Data

Newark, Tim *1961-*
Medieval warlords.
1. Warlords, 500-1500
I. Title
909.07

ISBN 0-7137-2234-7

Typeset by Graphicraft Hong Kong
Printed in Hong Kong by Colorcraft Ltd.

CONTENTS

PREFACE

In the court of a warlord, fear prevails. Fear to make your stomach churn. Fear to make any ordinary person want to run far away and be thankful to have escaped unscathed. It is the fear of physical violence. The warlord maintains his power through the threat of destruction and death. On anyone at anytime. He has no fear of inflicting violence. He is used to it and well practised in it. His is the rawest kind of power. To survive and succeed in the court of a warlord is to compete in an arena of perpetual terror. It takes an extraordinary person. Some are clever, some are tough, some are mad.

Tim Newark 1987

Dracula, prince of Wallachia, 15th century woodcut based upon a near contemporary oil painting.

FLAVIUS AETIUS

C.390−454

In the court of Alaric, Flavius Aetius grew strong in the skills of battle and politics. The Barbarian King of the Visigoths had demanded two hostages of noble background. They were the human guarantee in a treaty extracted from the Romans. Of the two teenagers delivered to his camp in northern Yugoslavia, Alaric took a liking to Aetius. It may have been that his father, Gaudentius, was a soldier of Barbarian blood that caused favour. Gaudentius had come from Scythia to rise in the Imperial army to the rank of Master of the Horse before being struck down by mutinous Gallic warriors. Now the boy looked to Alaric for fatherly guidance. His mother was an Italian of good family and vast wealth. It was from her that Aetius derived his hostage status. In the court of Alaric, however, it was the character of Aetius that impressed his hosts most of all. Alaric gave him weapons − sword, spear, and quiver − and encouraged him in the exercise of combat. Aetius grew fit and strong in muscle. And all the time, he watched and noted the ways of Alaric: learning the qualities that made a man a lord of warriors.

In AD 410, Alaric had had enough of Roman intrigue. He marched on Rome. The full facts of his entry into the Eternal City are unknown. Pagan chroniclers blame the catastrophe on the Christian neglect of the ancient temples and gods that had protected the capital for 800 years. Christians blamed the corrupt ways of their fellow men and saw the fall of Rome as a punishment of God. For the Romans in the city, they seem to have come to some compromise with the Barbarians as there was no great siege or bloody

assault. The gates of Rome were opened to Alaric and his gang of followers. Collectively known as the Visigoths, they were a force of Germanic and Eurasian freebooters, bandits, and runaway slaves. They were probably as closely related to their original tribal homeland beyond the Black Sea as the Romans. Travel weary, brutalised, and starved, these warriors were hungry for their slice of the greatest prize of all. Alaric was highly conscious of this: his power relied on their contented support. And yet he did not want to see Rome destroyed. He allowed his troops to satiate their wish for pillage, but he ensured the protection of the city's great buildings and holy places. After three days, strict order was restored. The reasoning behind this is obscure. Perhaps by showing his restraint and preserving the city, Alaric could use it as a bargaining point to gain a responsible position within the Imperial hierarchy. What Aetius did during these momentous events, we do not know. But we can be sure the young man observed with fascination the way Alaric maintained control of the situation, how he handled the politics, and how he exerted his authority over his warriors.

A crisis in food supply urged Alaric to quit Rome shortly after its conquest. The Visigoths rode south. At the toe of the Italian peninsula, they planned to sail to Sicily and then on to Africa. But Alaric grew ill and died. His warriors grieved. So that no one should know where their mighty leader lay, they buried Alaric beneath a dammed river and then let its waters flow over the grave and obscure it forever. Demoralised, hungry, and desperate for a legitimate place to settle, the Visigoths elected a warrior who could lead them towards compromise with the Romans. Athaulf was the chosen politician. He led his people into alliance with the Empire and married a Roman princess called Placidia. As part of the new spirit of friendship, the Visigoths returned their Roman hostages, among them Aetius.

At this stage, Aetius must have been aged about 20. He was a vigorous young man, but due to the death of his father, he may have lacked the patronage to gain him entry into a military career. Subsequently, and because of his brilliant track-record among the Visigoths, he was soon submitted as an Imperial hostage to another Barbarian people. This time it was the Huns. Dwelling beyond the Danube, and never having settled on Imperial territory, the Huns had not been Romanised to the degree of the Visigoths. The court into which Aetius was delivered was far removed from the Mediterranean palaces enjoyed by Alaric. Aetius could no longer expect such fine food or surroundings. The weather was harsh. One cannot help wondering whether Aetius had been involved in this onerous duty by an Imperial official who perceived in the competent and ambitious young man a possible threat. Perhaps it was hoped Aetius would never return.

The Huns were an essentially Turkish confederation of tribes. They fought in the manner of all Eurasian horsemen, placing a special emphasis and value on archery. To Aetius, this would not necessarily have been so alien as it was to other Romans or Germans. His father had come from Scythia and maybe it was Sarmatian and not Germanic Barbarian blood that pumped through his body. In the company of Hun horse-archers, he developed a fine sense of horsemanship and handled both lance and bow expertly. Later chroniclers remarked specifically on these skills acquired among the Huns. 'His intelligence was keen and he was full of energy,' wrote Renatus Frigeridus, 'a superb horseman, a fine shot with an arrow and tireless with the lance.' On the plains of Hungary, Aetius learned also the ability to withstand hardship. 'He bore adversity with great patience

11

and was ready for any exacting enterprise,' continued Frigeridus, 'he scorned danger and was able to endure hunger, thirst and loss of sleep.' Aetius' hardship among the Huns earned him a reputation for toughness that gained him the respect of common soldiers. He was building himself up.

In the second decade of the 5th century, the Huns were ruled by a King known as Charaton. It was at his court that Aetius became acquainted with the leading warriors of the horde. During feasts, Hun noblemen were fascinated to hear him recount his experiences with Alaric and during the sack of Rome. On hunting expeditions, Aetius may even have exchanged words with a similarly ambitious young man called Attila. It was Aetius' association with the older members of the horde, however, that were to prove invaluable in the future. He was securing a friendship with the Huns that would provide him with real military power. The Huns held no fear for him. Supposedly the most terrible of all the Barbarians, Aetius knew them as drinking partners. He knew how they thought and how they fought. This too was to be precious information in the future. Far from pining away in the wastes of the Barbaricum, Aetius emerged from the experience even stronger in character, connections, and knowledge. It was now time to direct his talents within the Imperial hierarchy.

The Empire that Aetius rejoined some time in the late years of the second decade was ruled by two Emperors. In the East, at Constantinople, the more vigorous and senior throne belonged to Theodosius II. In the West sat Honorius, constantly playing Barbarian against Barbarian, Barbarian against Roman, Roman against Roman. In 421, the elderly Honorius held his Emperorship jointly with his chief warlord, Constantius. Constantius had begun his career as an ordinary soldier and now, married to Placidia, the sister of Honorius, he had reached the peak of his ambition. It would not last long. For seven months, he enjoyed a life he had always dreamed of. He extorted great wealth from the most noble families of Italy. He constantly marvelled at the fortune and hard work that had brought him from frontier warfare in Dacia to an Imperial palace in Ravenna. Aetius may have been bored by such self-congratulation over lavish dinners in Ravenna and wondered whether he too possessed the ability to pursue this wild ambition. The sudden death of Constantius came as no surprise, but it aroused a sense of scandal in court circles, particularly regarding Placidia, who had never wanted to marry the soldier. 'So great had grown the affection of Honorius for his own sister,' rumoured Olympiodorus, 'that their immoderate passion and their continuous kissing on the mouth brought them under a shameful suspicion in the eyes of many people.' But politics soon brought an end to that. Fighting broke out in the streets of Ravenna between the Barbarian body-guard of Placidia and the Imperial guard of Honorius. Honorius banished Placidia and her son, Valentinian, to Constantinople in 423. A few months later, Honorius was dead.

The death of the Western Emperor was an irresistable opportunity for

An Emperor's *bucellarii*, his elite bodyguard. Usually Germanic warriors, they wore their hair long and wore torcs around their necks. Detail of a 6th century mosaic of Justinian from the church of St Vitale, Ravenna.

anyone bold enough to snatch it. With Placidia and her son in Constantinople and no other member of the Theodosian dynasty at hand, the Emperorship was wide open. Surprisingly, the throne was not seized by a military man, but a civilian. Nevertheless, John, chief secretary in the Imperial household, was backed by Castinus, Master of the Soldiers. He was supported also by Aetius, who had risen to the post of *cura palatii*, Governor of the Palace. It seems likely that Aetius achieved this rank through marrying the daughter of Carpilio, one time Head of the Imperial Household. Aetius had no wish to lose his job and for this reason may have felt compelled to throw in his lot with John.

In Constantinople, the death of Honorius meant that Theodosius was sole ruler of the Empire. He was loathe to give this up to Placidia. She insisted that her four-year-old son, Valentinian, was the true heir to the Western Empire. The usurpation of John, however, urged action. In addition, Placidia was not without power and influence of her own. Before her marriage to Constantius, she had been the wife of the Visigoth Athaulf. She admired the Germans and trusted her protection to a private army of Visigoth warriors. This gave her independence, and with all her connections built up over years in royal courts, she now called upon one of her most powerful friends. In north Africa, the warlord Boniface threatened to block grain shipments to Italy unless Valentinian was recognised as Emperor. Theodosius was forced to raise a Romano-Barbarian army led by the Alan officer Ardabur and his son Aspar. Alongside them rode Placidia with her gang of Visigoth retainers. Numbering as many as a few thousand, they were called *bucellarii*. The name refers to the dried bread which these hardy worriors received as rations. They were of high status: valued retainers, elite soldiers. They wore a kind of torc around their neck which perhaps symbolised their status and close relationship to their master. Like most Germanic warriors of the time, they wore their hair long, carried large oval shields and long spears.

Hearing of this force advancing towards Italy, Castinus set about adding troops to the court *bucellarii* of John. Seizing upon Aetius' contacts among the Huns, he sent the young man with a great sum of gold to their tribal leaders in Pannonia, now western Hungary. Aetius was to recruit the Huns and descend upon the rear of the Eastern Imperial army as it entered northern Italy. Castinus would then engage its vanguard. It was the chance Aetius had been waiting for: a demonstration of his worth and the military power he could call upon. On the Hungarian plains, he reawakened old friendships. The Huns gathered their horsemen for his gold. But events were moving too fast. John's troops had already captured Ardabur. Despite an apparent friendship between the two, the Alan general succeeded in undermining John's support from within to the extent that his army disintegrated and he was handed over to Placidia. While her son fidgeted beneath the robes of a Caesar, the Imperial mother watched with satisfaction as the usurper John was brought into the arena at Aquileia for execution.

14

Byzantine torc of gold on a bronze core, 6th century. Perhaps worn by a warrior of the *bucellarii*. Now in the British Museum, London.

Three days after John's execution, Aetius arrived in Italy with a force of Huns reputedly 60,000 strong.

It is possible that Aetius had not heard the news of John's death. But it would equally have been understandable if Aetius had realised the strength of the Eastern Imperial army and saw no point in identifying himself too strongly with the losing side, thus arriving too late. Nevertheless, in the new regime that would follow, Aetius had to prove from the start his strength. Therefore, he maintained his Hun army and confronted the Easterners. It seems unlikely that much blood was shed. Aetius did not wish

15

to waste his good relations with the Huns by losing them in a futile bloodbath. Instead, within weeks and after much negotiation, Aetius was reconciled with Placidia and the Huns were sent back to Hungary with a handsome payment. Aetius had successfully demonstrated his military potential. He was rewarded with the rank of *comes* – loosely 'count' – and command of Imperial forces in France. Castinus, who had supported John from the beginning, could not expect such generous forgiveness. He immediately escaped into exile.

Over the next four years, Aetius strengthened his ties with the Huns. He sent his own son among them as a hostage to learn the lessons he had. He successfully used Hun contingents to defeat the Visigoths in the south of France and the Franks in the north. The clash with the Franks was a typical case of maurauding Germans from beyond the Rhine border being driven back by the Empire. The struggle with the Visigoths, however, was an act of policing and serves as a useful introduction to explain exactly what Aetius' function was in France.

After the death of Alaric and the succession of Athaulf, the Visigoth leadership had sought to reach an agreement with the Romans. But there was dissension among the Goths and Constantius came down hard on them, expelling them from the prosperous cities of southern France. For a few years, they fought on behalf of the Empire in Spain against less acceptable Barbarians. In 418, Constantius recalled the Visigoths to southern France. He had another task for them. He signed a peace treaty with their leaders and settled them in Aquitaine around the city of Toulouse. It is interesting to note that such a move was not the wild roving of independent Barbarian warbands, but on the orders of a Roman with whom they were eager to deal. The military strength of the Visigoths was clearly inferior to that of the Romans. So why should Constantius invite the Goths back into France and give them the prime land of Aquitaine, for years the major source of grain for the Imperial army on the Rhine frontier? The fact that this territory was such a key agricultural area for the Empire holds the answer to Constantius' strategy. It is explained also by the fact that Aquitaine was not a borderland, but in the heart of France. The Goths had been settled there not to defend the frontiers of the Empire against outside Barbarians, as other tribes were. Aquitaine had to be protected from its own people: the discontented farmers and peasants of Roman France – the *Bacaudae*.

In 407, the *Bacaudae* of Armorica, now Brittany, had set upon their tyrannical land owners. They had taken their estates and thrown out Imperial governors. They set up an independent state and ruled the land for 10 years free of Imperial law and order. The organisation of the revolt, coinciding with a major Barbarian invasion, and its vast scale, demonstrated that this was no simple peasant revolt. Like other uprisings of the *Bacaudae* in the past, it may have begun with a mob of runaway slaves, army deserters, and bandits overthrowing several estates, but eventually it became a movement joined by small land owners and middle classes who

16

had suffered under the oppressive and corrupt wealthy estate owners and government officials. The revolt of 407 was the longest and most successful of all Bacaudic uprisings and profoundly terrified neighbouring landowners south of the Loire in Aquitaine. Campaigns against the *Bacaudae* were not easy. Like the Barbarians, the rebels avoided major confrontations, preferring to split up into a myriad of tight, controllable raiding parties: ravaging the enemy with relentless skirmishing and ambush and always gathering food and booty.

Slowly, Imperial forces managed to quell the most outrageous of the *Bacaudae* by 417. But to secure the estates of neighbouring territory, Constantius employed Barbarian auxiliaries. In 418, he installed the Visigoths south of the Loire around Toulouse. He bound the interests of the Barbarians to the settled business of land ownership by giving their chieftains their own estates. Thus the Visigoths had common cause with Roman aristocrats against the rebels. Generally, this proved successful and for many years the Goths kept the natives of Armorica in check. Sometimes there would be friction among the new allies: a rogue Visigoth ignoring the treaty of his lords, or, as in 425, the Visigoths taking advantage of the usurpation of John to attack Arles. On these occasions, Aetius had to intervene to keep the Visigoths in line. But on the whole, Theoderic, King of the Visigoths, and Aetius were united in the same task: the suppression of the Gallo-Roman lower classes. The defence of the Imperial frontier was, of course, still of vital importance. But frequently, it would be undertaken simply to secure Barbarians in the service of the Romans against the potential rebellion of the *Bacaudae*. This was the job of Aetius in France.

Such was his initial success as defender and policeman in the late 420s that Aetius was given the highest military rank of all: *magister militum*. Only Boniface, Count of north Africa, now possessed military power in the Western Empire to rival Aetius. But Boniface had problems of his own. He was a hard man, and in the late 420s, he was having a hard time. The Moors and African Barbarians he had successfully controlled for so long were beyond his authority. In 427, Boniface was recalled to Ravenna to explain his failures. He refused. A Western Imperial army was sent to bring him back. It was defeated and absorbed by Boniface. A second army of Goths was also subdued and Placidia agreed a peace. But events would not leave Boniface alone. In 429, the Vandals invaded Africa and Boniface proved unable to stop them. The time had come for the warlord to clear out and seek the grace of his patron Placidia. The Empress mother received Boniface with pleasure. Their dispute forgotten, she needed him to counter-balance the overwhelming presence of Aetius. Barbarian ambassadors were ignoring her and dealing straight away with Aetius. So powerful was he, that the Senate, the court, and reluctantly Placidia, had to acknowledge him as consul.

While Aetius campaigned in France, Placidia entertained Boniface and invested him with the office of *magister militum*. Aetius was furious, cut short his plans, and rushed back to Italy. Just south of Ravenna, at the 5th milestone beyond Rimini, the two warlords clashed. The word *pugna* used in one description of the battle suggests a minor combat, almost a duel. It was probably fought between the *bucellarii* of both men. In the struggle, Boniface was wounded but victorious, forcing Aetius to go into hiding, reputedly among the Huns. A few days later, Boniface died from his wounds. Aetius re-emerged with a contingent of Huns and defeated Boniface's son-in-law Sebastian. Aetius was now undisputed overlord of the entire Western Roman Empire. Placidia could do nothing but hope to earn his protection. A year later, Aetius was elevated to the honourable rank of patrician.

Having risen so far by the age of 40, Aetius contented himself with consolidating his power in France. Although happy to enjoy the high life of Ravenna and Rome, his heartland was most certainly in France. Policing the Visigoths and the *Bacaudae* consumed much time and effort. In 437, however, Aetius set his sight on controlling another potential threat. The Burgundians were a Germanic tribe settled in the southern Rhine region. 20 years earlier they had supported the Romano-Gallic usurper Jovinus. It may be that Aetius had intelligence suggesting they were involved in another attempted coup. Whatever the reason, Aetius and his lieutenant Litorius recruited a large number of Huns. They then hammered the Burgundians so devastatingly that the slaughter passed into Germanic legend. Gundahar, King of the Burgundians, his family, and 20,000 followers were all slain. Such was the devastation and terror wrought by the Huns that the incident formed the kernel from which the medieval German epic tale of the *Nibelungenlied* is derived. In the legend, the Huns were said to have been led by Attila and not Aetius. This is probably a mistake as chroniclers all name Aetius, while Attila only became leader of the Huns in 445. But it does suggest that the Burgundians may have been annihilated as a favour to the Huns who lived directly to their east, rather than specifically for Aetius.

For six years, the smashed Burgundians disappear from history. Then in 443, Aetius calls upon the survivors and settles them in the region of Savoy in South-east France. As with the Visigoths, the Burgundians were set up on prime Roman soil not to protect frontiers, but to secure the valuable Rhone Valley estates against the notorious *Bacaudae* among the western foothills of the Alps. In a similar endeavour in the early 440s, Aetius settled one group of Eurasian Alans in the Rhone Valley around Valence and another around Orleans as a buffer against unrest in Armorica. The Alans were regarded as particularly ferocious by their contemporaries. 'Aetius the Magnificent has been so enraged by the insolence of the proud Armoricans' wrote a contemporary 'that he punishes them for daring to rebel by giving Goar, the savage King of the Alans, permission to subdue them. Goar with a Barbarian's greed thirsts for Armorica's wealth.'

Between 437 and 439, Aetius had to contend with a major outbreak of Visigoth violence in southern France. Busy elsewhere, Aetius entrusted the

Byzantine Empress of the 5th century. Placidia was a powerful woman and made her son Emperor of the West.

command of a Hun contingent to Litorius. Liberating Narbonne from a
Goth siege, Litorius went on to further victories. 'At Snake Mountain,'
recorded Flavius Merobaudes, 'he surprised the enemy, as is his custom,
and killed a great many of them. Once the crowds of foot soldiers were
routed, he himself followed hard on the scattering horsemen and
overwhelmed those standing fast with his might and those fleeing with his
eager rapidity.' There is some confusion about who this passage actually
refers to and it may indeed describe Aetius in action. Initial Imperial
victories were lost in a morass of guerilla fighting. Outside Toulouse,
Litorius and his Huns were savaged by the Visigoths. Litorius died shortly
after from his wounds. Aetius took charge of the situation. From the scant
source material available, it appears the warlord either besieged the Goths
in Toulouse or attacked their fortified camps outside the city. Merobaudes
takes up the story.

'Barricades protected them, as did towers and ramparts piled on high
ground. There was a horde mixing Barbarian roughness with Roman
military ways. Warriors stood fortified with shields, brandishing spears and
swords and causing harm with arrows. On the one side there was the height,
impassable and bristling with defenders and ramparts. On the other side,
there was the bravery of our leader, destined to overcome war by skill. And
so, growling savagely with united strength, the warriors prepared to fight.
They cut down wood by the column. Fir was joined with fir to make siege
towers and when it was ordered to overtop the walls, it frightened the
opposing battlements with its height. At that time, there was no day

Visigoth gilt-bronze belt
buckle, 6th century.
Possibly from their
settlements in south-west
France. Now in the British
Museum, London.

without war and every night was spent in arms. Warlike arrows, destined to bring slaughter, found concealment throughout the dark shadows.' In this evocative though unclear passage, it appears Aetius finally led a night assault on the Goth defences. He triumphed and immediately concluded a treaty with Theoderic that reaffirmed the terms of the Visigoth settlement initiated by Constantius.

By the early 440s, Aetius was established as the chief defender of the Western Roman Empire, his power almost equal to the Emperor. Valentinian III was now of age to assume his Imperial responsibilities, but his mother Placidia still dominated the court and had found little way to curb Aetius' power. Aetius strengthened his position by surrounding himself with brilliant followers. Flavius Merobaudes, the author of many pretentious and obscure panegyrics to Aetius, took care of his master's propaganda in Rome and Ravenna. He probably wrote the inscription for the statue of Aetius erected by the Senate in the Atrium of Liberty at Rome. It proclaimed his important victories so far as those over the Burgundians and the Goths. The poet was rewarded with the rank of *patricius*. It seems to have gone to his head and brought out the most melodramatic myth-building when describing Aetius' childhood in the northern *Barbaricum*: 'scarcely had he planted his first steps in the snow over which he crawled than his hands sought a missile. He played with frozen rain and made a javelin out of ice.'

Other important followers of Aetius are described in the poems of Sidonius. There was the loyal Domninus: 'a renowned man who was content to the end with a single high office in the Imperial service just so long as he might follow one friend and cling to him in times of jeopardy. Not once but several times, the Imperial court strove with offers of the consulship to steal him from Aetius, but he stood firm – a greater man than those who received these dignities. A loyalty which no price could tempt came to be held more precious.' Aetius entrusted this loyal retainer with his treasury. Avitus followed Aetius because 'he had learned many a lesson from Scythian warfare,' that is, the warlord was experienced in Hun tactics. Avitus gained renown as a remarkable warrior: 'the Herulian found in him a match in fleetness, the Hun in javelin-throwing, the Frank in swimming, the Sauromatian in use of the shield, the Salian in marching, the Gelomian in wielding the scimitar. In the bearing of wounds, Avitus surpassed any mourning Barbarian to whom wailing means the tearing of cheeks with steel and the gouging of red traces of scars on his threatening face.' Avitus would become Emperor one day, but under Aetius he was content to serve as an envoy and lieutenant. By surrounding himself with such competent retainers, Aetius maintained his power as supreme warlord of the west.

In 445, Attila murdered his brother Bleda to become King of the Huns. Aetius was now over 50 and losing his old friends among the horde. He sent his eldest son, Carpilio, and other skilled ambassadors to make treaties with the new Barbarian ruler. The meetings were tense. Attila was no longer content for his people to be the sword and bow of Aetius. He had ambitions of his own. 'He fancied himself about to grasp the Empire of the world,' remembered one envoy. An old friendship could not be counted upon. In 448, Eudoxius, leader of the *Bacaudae*, found sanctuary among the Huns. Aetius asked for his extradition. It was not granted. But the two warlords did hold much respect for each other. They did business together. Above all, Attila seemed more interested in ravaging the Eastern Empire. The reputation of Aetius appears to have persuaded the Hun onto softer targets.

In 450, Theodosius, Emperor of the East, was dead. The succession was smooth and the new Eastern Emperor, Marcian, made it clear that no more tribute money would be paid to the Hun unless peace could be guaranteed. He did not fear Attila and would be happy to prove the point in battle. In the West, in that same year, the King of the Franks lay dead also. His succession was far from agreed. The King's younger son – a boy adopted by Aetius – went to the warlord for help. The elder son, not wishing to face

Sarmation horse-warrior. The Alans settled in France by Aetius wore similar scale armour. Marble stele found at Tanais in the Ukraine, now in the Hermitage, Leningrad.

Aetius alone, rode out of France to the court of Attila. An opportunity to crack open the West was welcomed. In the Imperial court at Ravenna, there was much diplomatic activity as well. Placidia was an old lady and would not last out the year, but before she died she witnessed one more attempt to break Aetius' power. According to the chroniclers, Honoria, sister of Valentinian and daughter of Placidia, sent her ring to Attila and pledged herself in marriage to him. The ridiculous though important offer had arisen out of a family squabble in which Honoria would give herself to Attila if he used his power to avenge an arranged marriage forced upon her. But was the real purpose behind this affair an attempt by Placidia and her son to recruit Attila as a new *magister militum*, the only hard man strong enough to oppose Aetius? In his correspondence with the Imperial court, Attila proclaimed he would advance into France on behalf of the Empire against the Visigoths, just as Aetius had done. Was Attila proposing himself as a new Defender of the West in return for the hand of Honoria and the possibility of inheriting the Imperial throne?

The new strength of the Eastern Empire, the Frank succession crisis, and the political offers of the Imperial court at Ravenna, all enticed Attila westwards. Throughout the remaining months of 450, the Huns prepared for a major campaign Attila called upon subject Eurasian and Germanic tribes that owed him service. The harvest was gathered and booty stored. Attila put pressure on the Imperial court. He demanded half of the Western Empire as his dowry on marriage to Honoria. Placidia had now died and Valentinian was left alone to decide what next. Attila's demands frightened him; he knew he could not handle the Hun. He caved in and begged Aetius for help. Aetius was well aware of the growing crisis and the threat of invasion. He mobilised his own forces. These were normally sufficient to quell any internal insurrection, but against a major external threat he was less well prepared. He had relied for so long on the Huns as his prime source of warriors, that he was now somewhat at a loss facing them as enemies. Who could he turn to?

The forces that Aetius eventually gathered all had a common stake in the defence of Imperial France. Essentially Barbarian, they had all been settled on Imperial territory in accordance with Roman treaties and now enjoyed their lives as Romano-Barbarian landowners. Aside from his own *bucellarii* and the private armies of Imperial magnates, Aetius was joined by the Visigoths, Burgundians, Alans, and Franks loyal to Aetius' adopted son. Curiously, the Armoricans are mentioned among the Western forces as well. Presumably, they refer to the *Bacaudae*. Perhaps the rebels realised their safety depended also on a concerted defence against Attila. In recognition of their service, Aetius acknowledged their presence as an independent contingent – a precedent they could call upon in future dealings with the Empire.

In the spring of 451, Attila and his horde crossed the Rhine into northern France. They rode for Metz and captured it. Then they cut through

Champagne until they struck Orleans with their battering rams. With this direct attack on his homeland, Sangiban, King of the Alans, lost his nerve and offered the city to the Huns. Just in time, Aetius and his allies arrived to prevent the loss. Outside the city walls, they set up earthworks and forced the Huns to withdraw. The Huns probably regrouped on the plains of Champagne, grassland admirably suited to their horsemanship and the confrontation they now anticipated. The scene was set for a battle whose exact location has forever remained a mystery. Generally called either the battle of *locus Mauriacus* or the battle of Chalons, it has most recently been accepted as taking place somewhere near the city of Troyes. Throughout the centuries, the battle at this location has been viewed as one of the decisive conflicts of history: Attila poised with a mighty army to crush the Western Empire in one final blow. It is little wonder the man standing in his way should have been called 'one of the last Romans', even though he was himself half Barbarian. It would be Aetius' greatest test.

On the eve of the titanic battle, Attila consulted his shaman for good omens. The man of magic examined the cracked shoulder blades of a sheep. The cracks did not augur well. The next day, Attila postponed the conflict until the afternoon, knowing that any disastrous withdrawal could be covered by night. The battlefield was a plain rising by a sharp slope to a ridge. When fighting eventually broke out, both sides sought to gain the advantage of this position. Horse-warriors from both sides rode up the slopes of the ridge. Aetius' horse-archers clad in mail and scale armour dashed forward. Joined by Visigoth nobles and their retainers, wielding lance and sword, they captured one side. Along the other slope charged the Huns with subject German tribes. A great struggle ensued for the crest of the hill. Archers let fly from afar while Germanic warriors thrust and hacked at each other. Theoderic commanded the Visigoths on the right wing of the allied Western army, while Aetius held the left. In the centre were the suspect Alans led by Sangiban. 'For he who has difficulties placed in the way of his flight,' wrote the chronicler Jordanes, 'readily submits to the necessity of fighting.' Attila positioned himself alongside his bravest warriors in the centre, with Ostrogoths and other Germans on his flanks. As the fight for the hill-top intensified, foot-soldiers joined the flailing crowd. Those Franks allied with Aetius hurled their famed *francisca* axes at the enemy before running into close combat.

Eventually, Aetius and the Visigoths gained the upper hand and threw the Huns back down the hill. Attila rode into the action and rallied his men with words of strength. 'Let the wounded exact in vengeance the death of his foe,' he bellowed. 'Let those without wounds revel in the slaughter of the enemy! No spear shall harm those who are sure to live. And those who are sure to die, Fate overtakes anyway in peace!' Warriors hammered each other until exhaustion or pain overcame them. Theoderic, the old and venerable chieftain, encouraged his Visigoths against their rival kinsmen, the Ostrogoths. They fought furiously and in the crush Theoderic was

thrown from his horse. Trampled in the chaos, he did not rise again. Enraged by such a loss, the Visigoths pushed back their adversaries and fell upon the majority of the Huns. Many Huns and their allies now took flight while Attila and the body of his army retreated behind the bulky wagons of their encampment. As dusk drew on, fighting became confused in the half-light, gradually ceasing as weary, wounded warriors stumbled back to their camps. During the night, it was claimed, the ghosts of the fallen continued the battle.

The next day, each side awoke to the dreadful spectacle of a battlefield heaped with the slain and wounded. Acccording to Jordanes, 165,000 warriors lay dead. Aetius and his followers felt certain they had won a great victory. But Attila still remained in the battle zone within his wagon fortress. 'He was like a lion pierced by hunting spears, who paces to and fro before the mouth of his den and dares not spring, but ceases not to terrify the surroundings with his roaring.' Aetius and his Germanic commanders decided to besiege the Hun camp. Attila had no great supply of food and according to Jordanes could make no successful counterattack as Aetius maintained a large number of archers within his camp. The Visigoths burned to avenge their dead chieftain. Attila prepared for a last stand. Determined not to be taken alive, he piled saddles within his wagons to form a fire upon which he would fling himself. But as the Visigoths grieved for their king and the Western army prepared itself for a final assault, Aetius had second thoughts. Why finish off the Huns? In the past, they had proved his most effective means of controlling the ambitions of the Germans in France. Attila would not rule the Huns forever and it seemed foolish to wipe out totally any possible renewal of the working alliance in the future. Besides, if the Visigoths were allowed to deliver the final blow, Aetius could not imagine restraining their demands for more land as a reward. Therefore, Aetius advised the son of Theoderic that others might sieze power in his homeland if he suffered badly in the forthcoming fight. Accepting this counsel, the Visigoths left immediately for Toulouse. Aetius used a similar argument to recommend the withdrawal of the Franks. Attila and his mauled forces were allowed to retreat westwards.

Aetius had won the greatest victory of his career. His reputation and power could stand no higher. He was truly Defender of the Western Empire. But was his judgement correct in letting Attila go? The discontent among his followers after such a defeat did not overthrow Attila. The Hun's grip on his warriors was too firm. Aetius had got it wrong. Attila considered his defeat a mere insult that determined him on a second assault on the West. In the spring of 452, the Huns descended on northern Italy, devastating Roman cities from Aquileia to Milan. The role of Aetius in this conflict is obscure. Strategically, he could not call upon the Romano-Barbarian forces he depended on in France. It seems likely he sacrificed the northern Italian cities in order to draw a line of defence north of Ravenna and south of the river Po. Throughout the summer, Aetius' horsemen harassed the plundering gangs of Huns. The previous year, the Po Valley had been ravaged by a terrible famine. The activities of the Huns did little to encourage the recovery of what paltry crops remained. Malnutrition struck Italians, Huns, and animals alike. Inevitably, disease broke out and Attila's horde could barely consider keeping hold of present conquests, let alone riding on to Rome or Ravenna. Attila's army collapsed as war bands began to make their way home. It was then that Aetius struck. Not with force, but with negotiation. The result was that Attila returned homewards beyond the Danube.

Attila's wagons may have been loaded with loot, but his second assault on the Western Empire had been a failure. He had not compelled the Romans to agree to any favourable treaty. They would not pay him tribute. They would not appoint him *magister militum*. The horde was devastated. And above all, Aetius remained the most powerful warlord in the Western Empire. A year later, Attila was dead and the Hun kingdom broke up. Contrary to legend, it may be that Attila was murdered by Hun chieftains outraged at their leader's costly failures. Perhaps Aetius had been right

about the Huns after all. It had taken two hard victories, however, not one.

To the followers of Aetius, it seemed remarkable that their lord should not wish to assume the Western Emperorship for himself. Valentinian was weak and posed no opposition. Instead, Aetius seemed content to rule as overlord of his pleasant estates in France. Besides, he knew from his youth the complications of usurpation, the possibility of provoking a vigorous Eastern Emperor. It didn't seem worth it. Anyway, everyone already acknowledged him as the most powerful man in the West. The conclusion of the war against Attila must also have worn out the warlord. He probably contemplated retirement. Such thoughts do not seem to have reassured

Attila the Hun. A demonic 16th century portrait at Certosa di Pavia. The Italians never forgave Attila for his destruction of their northern towns.

Valentinian. Without his mother and the removal of Attila, he could call upon no one to counter the power of Aetius. Suspicion irritated the Emperor beyond endurance. Eventually he could stand it no longer.

In September 454, Aetius was in Rome. He spoke with the Emperor. If Aetius had no Imperial aspirations for himself, he appears to have possessed them for his son, Gaudentius. Repeatedly, Aetius pressed a marriage between the young man and a daughter of Valentinian. The anxious Emperor could not bear the subject. He suddenly leapt up and cast wild accusations at the amazed warlord. All the resentment and fear Valentinian felt for the success of Aetius spurted out. 'Your desire for power will not end until you rule the Eastern Empire as well as the West.' Aetius tried to calm the nervous anger of the Emperor, but in the excitement Valentinian drew his dagger. He stabbed Aetius. The Emperor's chamberlain also drew a blade and cut the warlord down. Boetius, a close friend of Aetius, tried to prevent the tragedy, but was stabbed before he could save his master's life. To prevent the news of Aetius' death arousing the fury of the warlord's *bucellarii*, Valentinian blamed the murder on others and had them executed immediately. In the words of a shocked court minister, the Emperor had 'cut off his right hand with his left'.

The truth of this foolish, mad act did not remain long hidden from Aetius' most ardent followers. A few months later, one of the warlord's most loyal *bucellarii* completed the revenge. His name was Optila and fittingly he was a Hun. One morning, Valentinian rode into the Campus Martius to practise archery. As he helped the Emperor dismount, Optila plunged a knife into Valentinian's temple. When he staggered round to view his striker, Optila dealt him a second blow to the face that brought him down. Members of the Emperor's bodyguard stood by and watched. No one raised a hand to defend him. The assassination was an execution. The murder of a mighty warlord by a mediocre Emperor should end like this. Valentinian would not be missed. But the loss of Aetius was profound. He alone had maintained Imperial control over France, giving reality to the concept of a Western Empire. Without him, the individual Germanic settlements would soon rise to replace the old Roman province with a fragmentation of German kingdoms. And yet, despite the great military and political success of Aetius, there had been one warlord at the edge of his realm who had consistently defied him. Although the western provinces of north Africa were technically considered part of the Western Empire, Aetius seems hardly to have concerned himself with regaining Roman control over these regions. He led no campaign against the Vandals who now ruled them. Did Aetius' lack of interest in Africa reflect a sensible concentration of power or was he simply afraid? The answer may lie in the fact that the man who ruled the Vandals was Gaiseric: the other great warlord of the 5th century.

GAISERIC

Gaiseric was very clever. Everyone thought so. 'He was a man of deep thought and few words,' wrote Jordanes, 'holding luxury in disdain, furious in his anger, greedy for gain, shrewd in winning over the Barbarians and skilled in sowing the seeds of discord among his enemies.' As a young man just turned 20, his wit was already keen. He had won a following among the young aristocrats who hunted and raided alongside his father, King of the Vandals. But Gaiseric was a bastard, his mother anonymous among the King's concubines.

When the King lay dead, it was announced he had wished his eldest legitimate son, Gontharis, to succeed to his power. It was sensible to proclaim this. An eldest son, in any eyes, did have a strong claim to inheritance. To pass him over could cause considerable resentment and even split the tribe in bitter rivalry. 'But Gontharis was still a child,' wrote Procopius, 'and not of very energetic temper, whereas Gaiseric had been excellently trained in warfare and was the cleverest of all men.' Many agreed with this and sometime before AD 429, the boy Gontharis was removed. Gaiseric was undisputed King of the Vandals. 'The Germans choose their kings by birth,' wrote Tacitus, 'their generals by merit.' The tribal chieftains recognised the importance of a skilled warlord as their leader. They were preparing for a great adventure.

A more prosaic account of Gaiseric's kingship is given by Hydatius who simply states that Gaiseric assumed the throne after the death of his brother. Procopius' description is enriched by his own experience of court intrigue and murder a century later. Little changes, he says. One agrees. The Vandals were a Germanic confederation of tribes from beyond the Danube. In 406, their warbands in alliance with Alans and Suevei rode west, crossed the Rhine, and invaded France. It was not an entire people on the move. It was a lean, hard army of young men, leaving their homeland and families behind, searching for wealth, excitement, and a new life. After a few years of marauding, they crossed the Pyrenees into Spain in 409.

Clearly, the Roman Empire wasn't interested in hiring them as a useful buffer against peasant revolts. The Empire saw them for what they were: gangs of freebooters little interested in constructive settlement. In Spain, they grew up. The Empire employed Visigoths to harry and hunt them. Between battling with Romano-Hispanic landlords and rival Barbarian tribes, and then being hammered by the Visigoth Imperial Enforcers, the leading Vandals began to desire a land in which they could settle free from attack and free to raise a farm and family. They had grown tired of war, but war would not leave them alone.

Gaiseric understood the desires of his older comrades. Those raw, young men that had ridden into Spain 20 years ago now had the wealth they wanted – the comfortable Roman way of life they had dreamed of. And yet every year, they saw their brothers and the sons of their Spanish wives die in relentless feuding and raiding. Other Barbarians were hard on them all the time. The Vandals had never been and never would be invited to serve on behalf of the Empire. Their presence in Spain would not be tolerated and as long as other Barbarians were ambitious for Imperial employment, the Vandals would remain a target for every Imperial-backed marauder. Among Gaiseric's young contemporaries, the mood was different. They were hungry for triumph in war, hungry for adventure. Somehow, Gaiseric had to compromise the weary wishes of the older chieftains for settlement and the ambition of his young warriors for a new challenge.

At the beginning of the 420s, the Vandals had won a great victory against a Romano-Goth army led by Castinus. It had given them the confidence to establish their power in the ports of southern Spain, formerly Roman strongholds. There, they employed native ship-builders and practised the craft of seamanship. Soon, Vandal boats were riding the waves towards the Balaeric Islands of Majorca and Minorca, and the north African coast of the Roman province of Mauretania. Such seaborne raiding may have appealed especially to Gaiseric. At some stage, he had suffered a severe fall from his horse which left him permanently lame. Ever after, riding could not have been a favourite activity. On board ship, however, he could satisfy his need for the excitement of the raid. In lightly-built, oar and sail driven ships, Gaiseric speeded towards foreign coasts. While his retainers ensured his share of the booty, the young Vandal warlord gathered valuable in-formation. He already knew, as everyone knew in the Roman world, that the north African provinces were the chief suppliers of grain and oil to the Empire, especially Italy. But he also learned the strength and nature of the defences of this Imperial bread-basket. As king of the Vandals in 429, it seemed this was the direction his people should take. A final savage combat with the Suevi convinced him that the Vandals should cross the narrow strait of water into Africa.

Bearing in mind the situation in Spain, the seaborne success of the Vandals in the late 420s, and the accession of their first new King since 406, it seemed more than likely that the Vandals would move on to Africa. That said, many chroniclers insist that Gaiseric was invited into Africa by Boniface, chief Imperial warlord of the entire region. As *comes Africae*, Boniface had established his great power in Africa through force of arms and the patronage of Placidia, mother of the Western Emperor Valentinian III. 'Boniface was a heroic man,' wrote the contemporary Olympiodorus. 'He fought valiantly against the Barbarians, sometimes attacking with a few troops, sometimes with many, and occasionally even engaging in single combat.' He was a warlord with no fear of physical involvement in a fight. Olympiodorus records his willingness to bloody his hands. A landowner came to Boniface complaining that his lovely young wife was being seduced by one of the warlord's Barbarian followers. He bewailed the disgrace to his name and beseeched Boniface to set it right. In an action fitting of a young 'Godfather', Boniface made his way personally to the field in which the acts of seduction took place. He then surprised the Barbarian with the estate owner's wife and cut off his head. The next day, the landowner was called before Boniface and the decapitated head revealed. The man was shocked and amazed and forever in debt to Boniface. Thus, the warlord extended his power.

Throughout the early 420s, Boniface maintained a firm grip on the Roman province of north Africa, defending it against the incursions of the powerful Moorish tribesmen. By the middle of the decade, the situation was proving increasingly difficult. St Augustine, a friend and adviser, wrote to the warlord wondering at his lack of command. 'Who would ever have believed that Boniface, after becoming a Count of the Empire and Africa and with so large an army and so great authority, that the same man who formerly kept all these Barbarian tribes in peace by storming their strongholds and menacing them with his small band of followers, should now have suffered the Barbarians to be so bold, to destroy and plunder so much, and to turn into desert such vast regions once densely peopled?'

At the root of Boniface's military decline was a spiritual crisis. The death of this first wife affected Boniface profoundly. He had always wished to lead a more Christian life and now believed he was being punished for his violent career. In another letter from St Augustine, the bishop reassured Boniface that it was possible to be engaged in military service and please God. 'Some of us, in praying for you, fight against your invisible enemies. You, in fighting for us, contend against the Barbarians, our visible enemies. Think then, when you are arming for battle, that even your bodily strength is a gift of God. War is waged in order that peace may be obtained.' St

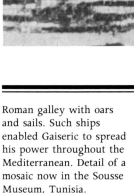

Roman galley with oars and sails. Such ships enabled Gaiseric to spread his power throughout the Mediterranean. Detail of a mosaic now in the Sousse Museum, Tunisia.

Augustine maintained that although it was acceptable for a warrior to fight, he must 'let the manner of his life be adorned by chastity, sobriety, and moderation. For it is disgraceful that lust should subdue him who man finds invincible and that wine should overpower him who the sword assails in vain.' It is the credo of the Crusader.

The common sense of St Augustine seems to have had little effect. At one time Boniface considered becoming a monk. But then, returning to earthly ways, he remarried. His wife was a Christian of the Arian faith, a heresy in Catholic eyes which believed that Christ was not of the same divine substance as God. The marriage shocked the Catholic Augustine. It also appears to have done little to prevent Boniface's continued military decline. 'What can I say of the devastation of Africa at this hour by hordes of African Barbarians,' Augustine exclaimed, 'to whom no resistance is offered, while you are engrossed with embarassments in your own circumstances and are taking no measures for averting this calamity?' He ends by saying he should not have dissuaded Boniface from the monastic life and he should now 'withdraw yourself so far as might be possible without prejudice to the public welfare from the labours of military service, and take to yourself the leisure you desired for a life in the society of saints in which the soldiers of Christ battle in silence, not to kill men, but to wrestle against the powers of spiritual wickedness, the devil and his angels'.

St Augustine was not the only Roman concerned with the breakdown in mind and performance of Boniface. In 427, he was recalled to the Imperial court at Ravenna to explain his failure. He refused and two armies were sent to get him. Surprisingly, considering the reason for which he was under attack, Boniface emerged triumphant from the assault. But at what cost? Prosper, Jordanes, Procopius, and John of Antioch all maintain that in his desperation, Boniface invited the Vandals into Africa to assist him against the Imperial forces from Italy. It was they who won him a respite from a displeased Emperor. And yet, almost as soon as Boniface had beaten off this immediate threat, there begins a war between him and the Vandals. Certainly both sides in this Roman civil war may have requested mercenaries from the Vandals, and Boniface through his wife may have had special connections with the Arian Germans. But it seems foolish of Boniface to invite Gaiseric and his followers into Africa without some formal treaty. What seems more likely is that Gaiseric was fully aware of the weakness of Boniface. When the Imperial forces came to battle with the rebel warlord, Gaiseric took advantage of the chaos and went ahead with his planned invasion. A fleet was constructed and while uncertainty dominated the Roman province, the Vandal King landed with followers reputedly 80,000 strong.

If the arrival of the Vandals in Africa was a mixed blessing for Boniface, depending on which story you believe, it was most definitely a catastrophe for the Catholic communities of Mauretania. The bishop Possidius described the dread felt by Catholics: 'They poured into Africa from across the sea in ships from Spain, a huge host of savage enemies arrived with every kind of weapon and trained in war. There were Vandals and Alans, mixed with one of the Gothic peoples, and individuals of various nations. They overran the country, spreading all over Mauretania and passing on to our other provinces and territories. There was no limit to their savage atrocities and cruelties. Everything they could reach they laid waste, with their looting, murders, tortures of all kinds, burnings, and countless other unspeakable crimes. They spared neither sex nor age, nor the very priests and ministers of God, nor the ornaments and vessels of the churches, nor the buildings.' It is from these outraged Catholic accounts that our concept of the Vandals as wild, wanton destroyers is derived. It was the fierce partisanship between Catholic and Arian that made the ensuing war in north Africa so bitter. One can compare it to the religious conflict of later centuries between Catholic and Protestant. Once when Gaiseric was embarking on a piratical expedition, the ship's pilot asked him where he was going. 'Against all who have incurred the wrath of God,' he boomed.

34

Soon after Gaiseric landed at Julia Traducta, now Tarifa, Boniface clashed with the pirate horde. As Possidius suggests, the Vandals included adventurers from other Germanic tribes as well as Spanish and Moorish marauders. The core of Boniface's army was his *bucellarii* – his private army. Their ranks thinned by fighting the Italian Imperialists, any gaps would have been filled by prisoners from the defeated Romano-Goths. To this may be added auxiliary forces of native tribesmen. Despite this array, Boniface was overwhelmed and the countryside lay open to Gaiseric. Boniface fell back to the fortified coastal town of Hippo Regius, now Bona. The Roman warlord probably felt compelled to draw his line of defence here as St Augustine was bishop of the community. Unable to capture the town in a direct assault, Gaiseric settled for a siege. Refugees from all around crowded into the walled town. Each day, they saw the Vandal siegeworks grow longer and stronger, depriving them even of their sea links. Catholic priests joined together in prayers for a hasty release, strengthening the resolve of the citizens against the Arians.

Three months into the siege of Hippo Regius, Augustine fell ill. The immediate presence of the Arians cannot have helped his state of mind. Within days, he was dead. The blow to the morale of the garrison was tremendous. Boniface probably felt directly responsible for the death of his venerable adviser. Eventually, messengers broke through the Vandal lines and after several months, a relief army was dispatched from Constantinople to Carthage under the leadership of Aspar. After 14 months, hunger and disease were ravaging the Vandals as much as the besieged inhabitants of Hippo. With the news of Aspar at Carthage and skirmishing along the coastline between the two cities, Gaiseric decided to relax the siege and enter into negotiations. Gaiseric still maintained the upper hand and wanted a good settlement. Boniface was allowed out of Hippo with his bodyguard, but having failed to stop the Vandals, his power in Africa was handed to Aspar and he sailed to Italy to be reconciled with his Emperor. Aspar established better relations with Gaiseric. He was an Alan by birth and Gaiseric's official title was 'King of the Vandals and Alans'. The two warlords exchanged gifts and ambassadors. Gaiseric was now established in Hippo, while Aspar maintained Imperial authority in Carthage. This division of the coastline was officially acknowledged in 435. Gaiseric obtained what every Barbarian chieftain desired: a treaty with the Empire legally accepting Barbarian claims. Using the face-saving convention of proclaiming the Vandals *foederati*, they were granted all regions west of Carthage. In reality, the Vandals would no sooner fight on the behalf of the Empire than anyone else. Gaiseric had won for his people an independent kingdom in north Africa, the first and only assault on this rich province by Germanic Barbarians.

The regime of Gaiseric was rigorously Arian. Catholic communities were disrupted and any priests refusing to perform the Arian service were banished or enslaved. It was also determinedly piratical. As in Spain, the

Moorish horsemen. The
Moors were ferocious
natives of north Africa,
but just as the Romans
had employed them,
Gaiseric recruited the
tribesmen into his armies.
Segment from Trajan's
Column, 2nd century.

Vandals augmented legitimate trading wealth with raids on prosperous neighbours. Hippo was an excellent port for such expeditions, all raiders paying a proportion of their booty to Gaiseric. In 437, the coasts of Sicily were plundered, pointing the way for future action. The presence, however, of Imperial forces in Carthage proved inhibiting. In 439, Gaiseric launched a surprise attack on Carthage. According to Hydatius, he captured it by trickery. Aspar had returned to Constantinople in 434 and the defences appear to have been soft. The shipyards of Carthage were a great prize for the Vandals. It enabled them to equip a fleet the equal of any navy possessed by the Romans or Byzantines. How the Empire ever allowed this catastrophe to occur must be one of the most monumental blunders of its history. In the hands of Gaiseric, Carthage once more rose as a great enemy of Rome. To celebrate the achievement, the Vandals made 439 the first year of a new calendar.

The ships the Vandals possessed in Carthage were the same as those employed by the Empire throughout the Mediterranean. The general trend at this time was for fast, light ships. The massive, several banked galleys of previous centuries had been replaced by *dromon* type craft. The name meant 'racer' and was applied to galleys of one bank of oars with each rower working one oar. It was only later in the Byzantine navy of the 10th century that *dromon* applied to more massive warships. In Procopius' 6th century descriptions of *dromon*-type ships, they emerge as galleys of the cataphract kind, that is, they have high parapets or a raised deck overhead from which hung a screen covering the oar-ports. Thus, the rowers were protected against arrows and other missile weapons. Cataphract means 'totally fenced in'. This was vital as an average crew of 30 to 35 men functioned as both rowers and warriors. A naval historian has estimated that such ships were 50 feet long, had a 17 tons' displacement, 22 oars, and a maximum speed of 6.3 knots. This may be an underestimate of size, but clearly they were light, fast ships which suited very well the sudden piratical attacks of the Vandals. To increase speed when not under attack, a *dromon* possessed mast and sail. The earliest evidence of the lateen sail – the triangular sail with the whole of its leading edge attached to a yard – is vague, but it was pioneered in north Africa by the Arabs in the 7th century and it seems likely it was known among Moorish sailors of previous centuries. Bigger warships were present in the Imperial navy, but on the whole, there appears to have been little need for large standing navies of multi-banked galleys. The *dromon* was the fighting ship of the 5th century.

Already by the spring of 440, a vast fleet manned by Vandals, Alans, Goths, Romano-Barbarians, and Moors set out from Carthage for Sicily. With the loss of Africa, this island had become a principal supplier of oil and grain to Italy. Now its coastal towns were looted, Palermo besieged, and swollen ships returned to the court of Gaiseric. The Eastern Empire responded by sailing a powerful fleet into Sicilian waters in 441 under the command of the Romano-Goth Areobindus. But a major invasion of the

Balkans by the Huns, and the threat of a Persian attack, forced the ships homeward before they could achieve anything. As a result, the Western Emperor thought it more astute to prevent any further assaults with a treaty. In 442, there was no face-saving. Gaiseric was acknowledged as an independent ruler. He was granted control of the most valuable land around Carthage and Hippo, as well as the land far to the west that dominated the straits of Gibraltar. Egypt and eastern North Africa remained part of the Eastern Empire and beyond Vandal ambitions.

Within his kingdom, Gaiseric settled his foremost retainers on the rich villa estates around Carthage, thus keeping a close eye on them. The transformation of the region from Roman to Vandal only affected the upper classes of society. The great Imperial estate holders were dispossessed, if they had not already fled, while everyone else – traders, farmers, and peasants – continued their lives as before, resenting the corruption and exploitation of their Vandal rulers only as much as they had that of the ruling Romans. The exception to this continuity was, of course, the Catholic priesthood. They suffered terribly.

With his powerbase acknowledged and secure, Gaiseric emerged as a statesman as well as a warlord. 'The occupier of Libya has dared to tear down the seat of Dido's kingdom and has filled the Carthaginian citadel with northern hordes,' announced the Imperial poet Merobaudes. 'But since then, he has taken off the garb of the enemy and desired ardently to bind fast the Roman faith by more personal agreements, to court the Romans as relatives of himself, and to join his and their offspring in matrimonial alliance.' It was true. A marriage was proposed between Eudocia, daughter of the Western Emperor, and Huneric, son of Gaiseric. It was a great honour for a Barbarian leader. But whose idea was it? It seems possible that Aetius, chief defender of the Western Empire, realised the impossibility of defeating the Vandals in battle. His forces were committed to France and he saw the betrothal as the best hope for peace. From another point of view, it could be that the Emperor Valentinian desired a powerful alliance with a Barbarian force that would counter-balance the considerable power of Aetius with his Huns and Goths. Whose ever idea it was, the political result must have pleased them both for it led to Gaiseric's first major political blunder.

Huneric was already married to a Visigoth princess when the Imperial offer of marriage arrived. Gaiseric had to make his son free again. They contrived that the poor Visigoth girl should be accused of trying to poison the Vandal king. As a punishment for the fictional crime, her ears and nose were cut off and the disfigured girl was sent back to her father in Toulouse. This savagery enraged the king of the Visigoths. He swore revenge. From then on, the Vandals and Visigoths were the bitterest of enemies. Needless to say, the proposed marriage between Vandal and Roman fell through and Gaiseric was left only with the addition of a major enemy. Nevertheless, Gaiseric seems to have been assured of Roman friendship and the remaining decade saw little serious conflict between them. Gaiseric sat back and enjoyed the considerable fruits of his African estates. He was in his middle 40s and may have felt he had attained all he wished. 'He is sunk in indolence,' wrote Sidonius of Gaiseric. 'And thanks to untold gold, no longer knows aught of steel. A drunkard's heaviness afflicts him, pallid flabbiness possesses him, and his stomach, loaded with continual gluttony, cannot rid itself of the sour wind.' Certainly, Gaiseric was enjoying himself, but he was far from slowing down. The events of 455 would demonstrate this only too clearly.

In 454, Aetius was murdered by a suspicious Emperor. The next year, Valentinian was stabbed to death by avenging *bucellarii*. The story goes that Eudoxia, the widow of the Emperor, was then forced to marry Maximus, usurper of the vacant throne and involved in her husband's assassination. To revenge herself against Maximus, Eudoxia wrote to Gaiseric, inviting him to take possession of Rome. No such invitation was needed. Gaiseric's peace treaty had been with Aetius and Valentinian. They were now dead, so was the treaty. Vandal agents reported the weakness of a new regime trying to establish itself. Gaiseric was angered by the news that Maximus had hurriedly married his son to Eudocia, for so long promised to Huneric. For over 10 years, the Vandal fleet had been built up, awaiting a major expedition. It was now cut loose.

As the Vandal fleet sailed along the coast of Italy in 455, none challenged it. Maximus could not rely on the support of the army and by the time the Vandal sails came in view of the port of Rome, he was on the road to Ravenna. An angry Roman crowd recognized him and stoned him to death. Unopposed, Gaiseric entered Rome. He was met by Pope Leo I who persuaded the Vandal King from fire and slaughter, to content himself solely with plunder. For two weeks, Gaiseric stayed in the Imperial palace. The Empress Eudoxia, her two daughters, Eudocia and Placidia, and Gaudentius, the son of Aetius, all became his prize prisoners. To this was added all the treasures and Imperial insignia of the palace, loaded on his ships to adorn his palace in Carthage. Part of the gilded roof of the Temple of Jupiter Capitolinus was removed. The invaluable vessels of Solomon's Temple, taken by Titus from Jerusalem, passed on to the Vandals. Gaiseric was master of the Western Mediterranean. He could have seized the Emperorship but probably considered it more trouble than it was worth. Instead, he finally had the satisfaction of seeing his son married to the daughter of a Roman Emperor. After their brief stay, Gaiseric and the Vandals sailed back to their stronghold in Carthage.

Gaiseric's position among his own people was unassailable. His overwhelming success encouraged autocratic power. As did a conspiracy among some Vandal lords which was bloodily suppressed. In response, Gaiseric favoured a government in which the old tribal aristocracy was replaced by officials who owed their position to his patronage and not their birth. This allowed Gaiseric to employ the talents of Romans and non-

Vandals. Later, he passed a law in which succession to his throne was restricted to the royal family and not subject to the ancient Germanic custom of election. Such was his authority that Gaiseric's will was accepted with little struggle. According to Procopius, Gaiseric organized his warriors into 80 companies commanded by captains called *chiliarchs*, which means 'leaders of 1000'. This force included all Gaiseric's Vandal and Alan supporters, but increasingly, as time passed and many Germans retired to the good life, the largest proportion consisted of black Moorish tribesmen. These were either paid recruits or warriors delivered as tribute by subject chieftains. If Gaiseric could assert his control over half the Roman Empire, then one can assume the majority of Moorish kingdoms gave him few problems. 'Now Gaiseric arms mine own flesh against me,' bemoans the personification of Africa in a poem by Sidonius. 'I am being cruelly torn under his authority by the prowess of mine own. Naught does he perform with his own arms. Gaetulians, Numidians, Garamantians, Autololi, Arzuges, Marmaridae, Psylli, Nasamones – it is these that make him feared.' These Moorish tribes – real and imagined – had indeed become the key strength of Gaiseric's army. They accompanied him to Rome and they fought in every succeeding campaign.

In the years following the sack of Rome, the Vandals relentlessly plundered Sicily and the coasts of southern Italy. Avitus, a new Emperor of the West, applied to Constantinople for help. But there, Aspar was dominant and his old relations with Gaiseric, as an Alan and an Arian, discouraged him from taking any direct action against the Vandals. Avitus turned to his chief warlord Ricimer. The half Suevian, half Goth Ricimer had a couple of successes against the Vandals, but on the whole they proved elusive. 'Unconquerable Ricimer,' wrote Sidonius, 'to whom the destiny of our nation looks for safety, does barely drive back with his own unaided force the pirate that ranges over our lands, that ever avoids battle and plays a conqueror's part by flight.' Sidonius goes on to describe one of the few Roman victories against a Vandal raid. He recalls a skirmish in Campania in southern Italy, sometime in 458 at the beginning of the reign of another new Emperor, Majorian.

'A savage foe was roaming at his ease over the unguarded sea. Under

Germanic gilt-bronze belt fitting inlaid with garnet and glass, 5th or 6th century. Possibly Vandal, found in the Near East, now in the British Museum, London.

southerly breezes he invaded the Campanian soil and with his Moorish soldiery attacked herdsmen when they dreamed not of danger. The fleshy Vandals on their oarsman's benches waited for the spoil, brought to them by their Moorish captives. Suddenly, the warriors of Majorian had thrown themselves between the two enemy hosts on the plain separating the sea from the hills. The plunderers fled towards the mountains and cut off from their ships became the prey of their prey. Then the Vandal pirates were aroused and massed their forces for battle. Some landed their well-trained horses in light rowing boats, some donned meshed mail as black as themselves, some readied their bows and arrows made to carry poison on the iron point and wound doubly with a single shot. The dragon standard sped hither and thither in both armies, its throat swelling as the zephyrs dashed against it. The trumpet's deep note sounded with a terrific blast and was greeted with shouts. From everywhere a shower of steel came down. A hurtling javelin struck one man down in the dust. Another man was sent spinning by the thrust of a spear. One gashed by a blade, another by a lance, fell headlong from his horse. A warrior swept off part of a foeman's brain and part of his helmet together, cleaving the hapless skull with a two-edged sword wielded by a strong arm. As the Vandals began to turn and flee, carnage took the place of battle. In their panic, the horsemen plunged into the water and swam back in disgrace to their boats from the open sea.'

After this minor victory, swollen by the hyperbole of Sidonius, Majorian initiated the building of a great fleet and the recruiting of a mighty army. In France, he obtained recognition from the Visigoths and Burgundians, many of whom joined the Suevi, Huns, Alans, and other Barbarians forming his army. In 460, Majorian moved swiftly into Spain and on to Africa. Apparently, the Imperial force was so strong that immediately Gaiseric thought it more prudent to suggest a treaty. Majorian refused. Gaiseric instructed his Moorish warriors to lay waste Mauretania and poison the wells in order to hinder the Roman advance. Then, through a combination of treachery and the action of his most able buccaneers, several of Majorian's ships were captured in their port. With both advance on land and sea devastated, Majorian was forced into peace talks. He left the continent a failure, the defeat bringing a speedy end to his reign.

The accession of a new Western Emperor in 461 gave Gaiseric the excuse to break all previous treaties and resume his raiding on Sicily and Italy. 'They did not lightly attack the cities in which there chanced to be a military force of Italians,' wrote Priscus, 'but seized the places in which there was not a rival force. The Italians could not bring assistance to all parts accessible to the Vandals, being overpowered by their numbers and not having a naval force.' Every year, the Vandals grew ever more daring and ever more rapacious. Sardinia, Corsica, and the Balearic Islands all came under their control. In 467, Gaiseric went too far. It may not have been his fault – more the greedy action of a rogue Vandal pirate. Territory of the Eastern Empire was violated by a raid on southern Greece. The Eastern

Vandals clash with Romans. Although portrayed as northmen, it seems the majority of Vandal armies in the mid 5th century were composed of black Moorish warriors. From Ward Lock's *Illustrated History of the World*, 1885.

Emperor Leo was outraged. Despite the reluctance of Aspar, Leo urged retaliation and sought closer links with the Western government. Leo obtained the Western Emperorship for his candidate, Anthemius, with the backing of Ricimer. At last, it seemed as if both halves of the Empire would move against the Vandal King. In response, Gaiseric declared his treaty with the East void and allowed his ships to attack Yugoslavia and Greece. Even Alexandria in Egypt was not safe.

Vandal horseman lassooing a stag. The majority of Vandals in north Africa became a ruling elite over the native population. Mosaic from Carthage, c.500, now in the British Museum, London.

Sixty five thousand pounds of gold and 700 pounds of silver were poured into the equipping of 11,000 ships and 100,000 warriors. It was the most ambitious fleet ever sent against the Vandals and brought Leo near to bankruptcy. In 468, the fleet sailed from Constantinople. The Byzantine commander was Basiliscus. Not the most competent of generals, his appointment may have been urged by Aspar who still favoured good relations with the Vandals. The Byzantines were joined by the Italian fleet of Marcellinus. Together, they designed a common strategy: a three-pronged attack. Basiliscus took the major part of the Eastern fleet direct to Carthage. Heracleius, a Byzantine general, obtained auxiliaries in Egypt and then sailed for Tripoli where he would disembark and march by land to Carthage. Marcellinus, in the meantime, used his Italian fleet against the Vandals in Sardinia. Sailing into Sicilian waters, Basiliscus confronted a Vandal fleet and sent 340 enemy galleys to the bottom of the sea.

Set sea battles were rare in the 5th century and something the Vandals avoided whenever possible. The classic ram and board warfare of the ancient Mediterranean still pertained. But greater emphasis was placed on fire-power, as the proliferation of cataphract-type ships suggests. A hail of archery preceded any encounter. To this was added the shot of catapults and *ballistae*: their stones and iron weights were intended to hole a galley.

Vandal nobleman hunting with hound. His horse is branded with an Arian cross. Mosaic from the Vandal capital at Carthage, c.500.

Greek Fire was a feared weapon of the Byzantine navy, but it is uncertain whether this was widespread in the 5th century. Other bizarre missiles were claypots filled with quicklime or serpents and scorpions. The Byzantines also invented a device for filling an enemy ship with water.

Marcellinus had success in Sardinia and regained control of the island with no great difficulty. Heracleius landed with a considerable force in Tripoli, confronting a Vandal army along the Libyan coast. The battle between the two land forces probably took the form of later Vandal conflicts described by Procopius. The true Vandal warriors, by this time assuming an elite rank in Gaiseric's armies, were all horsemen. Like most warriors of Germanic blood and culture, they maintained a prejudice against horse archery, believing it more manly to enter into close combat as soon as possible with sword and spear. Under the command of their *chiliarchs*, the Vandal horsemen usually gathered on the flanks of an army. In the centre were the Moors. They travelled on camel back and if the fighting was to be an aggressive, skirmishing attack, they remained in the saddle. If they were to face a professional, regular army, they may have taken a more defensive stance. On these occasions, they dismounted and incorporated their camels into a phalanx in which they stood with spears, javelins, and shields amid the legs of their animals. Horsemen unfamiliar with the sight and smell of Moorish camels could be thrown into disorder. Against Heracleius, however, they had little effect. The Moorish javelin shower, the camel phalanx, and the elan of the Vandal horsemen failed to break the Imperial force. The Byzantines counterattacked, delivering a cracking punch with their hordes of Barbarian horse-archers, among them many Huns. Following this victory, Heracleius captured several towns and marched confidently towards Carthage. With all three forces of the Empire closing in on him, Gaiseric must have feared for his survival. Now was the time for his famous intelligence.

Basiliscus and his fleet anchored at the Promontorium Mercurii, now Cape Bon, not far from Carthage. The Vandal capital lay vulnerable. Immediately, Gaiseric sent ambassadors to the Imperial warlord to gain a little more time. His envoys promised Basiliscus great wealth and according to some chroniclers this may have purchased an armistice. While the Byzantines discussed when to finish off the Vandal menace, Gaiseric ordered a fleet of old galleys and filled them with brushwood and pots of oil. When the wind rose and the moon was obscured by cloud, the hulks were towed towards the Imperial mooring. Against the black sky, Byzantine guards observed Moorish sailors darting to and fro with blazing torches on the boards of the old ships. Too late the alarm was sounded to the accompaniment of an explosion of flames. The ocean wind pushed the fireships further towards the Imperial fleet. The fire leapt from galley to galley. By morning, Basiliscus had lost the campaign. His burnt-out fleet drifted back to Sicily, harassed by Moorish pirates.

In Sicily, it was hoped Marcellinus would save the situation. But an assassin, perhaps a Vandal agent, killed him. Any further expeditions against Africa were abandoned. Heracleius heard the news just in time to retrace his steps eastwards. Basiliscus returned to Constantinople but public outrage was so intense he was forced to seek sanctuary in St Sophia. For the Eastern Emperor, the failure was a crisis politically and economically. For Gaiseric, it was a remarkable victory. The combined might of both Empires had been thrown against him and he had emerged triumphant. His followers regarded the old man with awe. He was the strong man of the Mediterranean.

Gaiseric maintained pressure on the Empire through diplomatic channels as well as war. In France, Imperial authority had retreated to the extent that the Franks, Burgundians, and Visigoths all governed independent kingdoms. Gaiseric capitalised on this. By the time a new King rose to the Visigoth throne, previous antagonism between the two peoples appears to have been overlooked in the pursuit of political expediency. 'Eurich, King of the Visigoths, beheld the tottering Roman Empire and reduced Arelate and Massilia [in southern France] to his own sway,' recorded Jordanes. 'Gaiseric enticed him by gifts to do these things, so as to hinder plots which the Emperors Leo and Zeno had contrived against him. Gaiseric also stirred the Ostrogoths to lay waste the Eastern Empire and the Visigoths the Western, so that while his foes were battling in both Empires, he might reign peacefully in Africa.' Gaiseric funded and patronised terrorism throughout the Mediterranean. Jordanes even alleges the Vandal was behind Attila's invasion of France in 451. 'When Gaiseric learned that Attila was bent on devastation of the world, he incited Attila by many gifts to make war on the Visigoths, because he was afraid that Theoderic, their king, would avenge the injury done to his daughter.'

46

Germanic gilt-bronze disc brooch with glass inlay, Vandal, 5th century. Found in Bone, Algeria.

The early 470s saw some major changes within the Imperial hierarchy. In 471, Aspar was murdered by the Emperor Leo. In 472, Ricimer died. In 474, Leo died. All these events encouraged major assaults on Italian and Greek coasts. The butchering of Aspar and his family particularly angered Gaiseric, revealing the special relationship they enjoyed. The new Eastern Emperor Zeno tried to bring a negotiated end to the raids. His embassy to Carthage met with surprising success. It may have been the incorruptible quality of Severus, the leading ambassador, that so impressed Gaiseric. Used to buying the services of Imperial agents, the Vandal king presented him with rich gifts and money, but Severus refused. 'In place of such things, the reward most worth while for an ambassador is the redemption of prisoners.' In reply, Malchus records that Gaiseric acquiesced. 'Whatever prisoners I, along with my sons, have obtained, I hand over to you. As for the rest who have been portioned out to my followers, you are at liberty to buy them back from each owner, but even I would be unable to compel their captors to do this against their will.'

In addition to the freedom of prisoners, Severus obtained a truce in the Vandal persecution of Catholics. In his old age, Gaiseric appears to have wanted to impress the rest of the Mediterranean with his tolerance and civilisation. In return, the Eastern Emperor recognised the full extent of the Vandal kingdom, including all of western Africa, the Balearic Islands, Corsica, Sardinia, and Sicily. Gaiseric was content with peace. Gazing out from his palace across the Mediterranean, he considered his life. He had observed the Western Roman Empire break up into numerous Germanic kingdoms. He had humbled a dizzying succession of Emperors, both West and East. He had outlived all the great warlords: Aetius, Attila, Theoderic, Ricimer, and Aspar. In 476, he witnessed the deposition of the last Emperor of the Western Roman Empire. The next year, Gaiseric was dead.

In an age of relentless assassination, it is significant of Gaiseric's stature among his own people that he was allowed to die a natural death. In his will, he proclaimed his eldest son, Huneric, as successor. But no one could hope to continue the success of Gaiseric. Within a few years, the Moors revolted and the great kingdom began to crumble. No one could command the respect Gaiseric had won. Just over 50 years later, the Vandal kingdom was crushed by the Byzantines and the last Vandal King taken as prisoner to Constantinople. The Vandal kingdom of north Africa was the creation of Gaiseric, the personal realm of a warlord.

AN LU-SHAN

The smell of sweating folds of flesh was overwhelming. The giggles of the harem girls became strained under the weight of the fat man's massive bulk. They carried him on through corridors in the Imperial Palace. Finally, before the Emperor's consort, Yang Kuei-fei, they slammed down their ridiculous burden. Yang screeched with laughter. Tears ran down her face. The fat man bubbled with laughter too. The obese warlord An Lu-shan was dressed in nothing but a huge baby's diaper. When the amusement subsided, An was lifted nearer Yang. She would adopt the fat man as her son. Against a background of sniggering, the ceremony proceeded. Everyone knew it was only a game, not an official adoption, but everyone also knew the joking meant that An Lu-shan had the intimate friendship of the most powerful heads of the Chinese Empire. Not bad for a half-breed Barbarian. The fat man was laughing indeed.

An Lu-shan was half Turk, half Iranian. Such people, like all nomadic tribesmen beyond their frontier, were considered Barbarians by the Chinese. He was born around AD 703 in the region of Bukhara in Sogdiana, present day Uzbekistan, Soviet central Asia. He came from a good family. His mother was descended from a noble Turkic clan. Some say she was a shaman and told fortunes. His father died while he was still a child. He may have been a warrior: Lu-shan is believed to be a Turkic word meaning 'warfare'. His mother continued to mix with the Turkic military elite and eventually remarried the brother of a warlord.

In previous centuries, the Turks of central Asia were famous as metalworkers. They were employed by the Juan-Juan, making the blades that made this tribe so terrible to the Chinese of the Han dynasty. Around the middle of the 6th century, the Turks rebelled against Juan-Juan overlordship. Bumin, their leader, asked for a Juan-Juan princess in marriage. The overlords replied that no princess could marry a blacksmith slave. In alliance with Chinese warriors, the Turks smashed the arrogant Juan-Juan and Bumin became warlord of the steppes. His descendents expanded Turkic rule both east and west. Raiding campaigns cowed the Chinese. But clever Chinese diplomacy and internal disputes eventually split the Turks into eastern and western Khanates. The Turks revived in the early 7th century when rebellion in China produced the T'ang dynasty. Yet the strength of the early T'ang Emperors meant an inevitable end to the eastern Turks. By the beginning of the 8th century, the Turks had fought back and were again the prime enemies of the Chinese Empire along its western and northern borders. Their eastern Khan Qapaghan had even been accepted by many western Turks as their leader, so in theory the Turks were once more united. Such a powerful alliance could not be maintained. In 716, Qapaghan was lured into a trap by rival Turkic tribesmen. His head was presented to the Chinese. The chaos following his assassination convulsed the Turks. Their lordship of the steppes was saved by a coup. A bloody purge of Qapaghan's supporters followed. Many Turks fled across the Chinese border, among them the An tribe and the teenage Lu-shan.

The fugitives were received by the son of a friendly Turkic warlord, a deputy commander of a Chinese frontier post. The banishment had been traumatic. In the aftermath, Lu-shan and other members of the An clan swore to become brothers. They had helped each other escape and would help each other in the future. Lu-shan formally took the surname of An. The An fugitives had arrived with little wealth and were forced to seek various means of income. One chronicler maintains that An Lu-shan became a notorious bandit. Another account is more prosaic. Because of his knowledge of several Barbarian languages, he made a living as a middleman, a broker, in the frontier markets set up by the Chinese government for trading with the Barbarians. Apparently Lu-shan's income was not enough. He was caught stealing sheep. The trembling 20-year-old was brought before Chang Shou-kuei, the military governor of Fan-yang on the north-east border. Lu-shan was forced to kneel. The executioner raised his club. Lu-shan screamed: 'Does the great lord wish to destroy the Barbarians? Why kill a brave warrior?' Shou-kuei stopped the execution. Lu-shan was a stout, strong young man with extensive knowledge of the Barbarians. He could be useful. Shou-kuei employed him as a scout.

On the north-east Chinese frontier, beyond the Great Wall, Khitan and Hsi Mongolian tribesmen were causing great trouble with their raiding. In the spring of 733, they defeated a Chinese army and killed its leader. Shou-kuei took command and Lu-shan soon found himself involved in cavalry skirmishes with the enemy. He proved adept at such fast-moving

operations, confirming Shou-kuei's faith in him. He became Shou-kuei's chief lieutenant and a successful battlefield commander. Warfare at this time consisted simply of raid and counter-raid, terrorism and counter-terrorism. Gangs of horse-archers on both sides fought to maintain the authority of their masters over the borderland. Ordinary people suffered from both sides, while the warriors grew rich in booty and reputation. The Chinese recruited great numbers of Barbarian horsemen for their frontier armies. They were called the 'claws and teeth' of the Empire. As was true in most nomadic armies, the horsemen were organised in units of multiples of 10. The Chinese believed the high martial skills and fervour of such warriors could only be aroused by charismatic leadership. Lu-shan appears to have possessed this quality. Chang Shou-kuei adopted him as his son.

Relations between An and Chang were not always friendly. Lu-shan's tough stoutness was already beginning to turn to flab and Shou-kuei frequently berated him for his fatness. Lu-shan feared Shou-kuei as much as admired him and in his presence he was careful not to gorge himself, even though he might be feeling ill with hunger. More serious problems also rocked Lu-shan's ambitious career. In 736, the Hsi and Khitan tribesmen rebelled against Chinese overlordship. Shou-kuei was away visiting the capital. Lu-shan had to face the raiders alone. He suffered a severe defeat with many casualties. Shou-kuei was furious. He accused Lu-shan of inadequate preparation and overconfidence. He requested permission from the Emperor for his lieutenant's execution. It was granted. But the anger subsided. The bad sense of killing a major commander saved Lu-shan's life. He was temporarily reduced to civilian status. By the end of the year, he was back in the saddle.

China in the early 8th century was still a vast unified Empire. But hair-line cracks were beginning to open. In the previous century, the T'ang military system had been based on the *fu-ping* organisation. This depended on an army of militia men. Serving in rotation, they spent some time at a frontier post, some time guarding the Emperor at the capital, and some time tending to their farm work. Because the militia men were committed to military service until the age of 60, many came from the privileged classes. A high standard of professionalism and loyalty could be expected from them. The organisation also meant that the armed forces tended to be divided between a large number of small units scattered around the country, moving around every three years, and a concentration of Imperial guards at the capital. The political advantages of centralised control of the army are obvious. The part-time nature, however, of the militia meant that it was best suited to planned campaigns, so that the men need not be away from their farms for too long, rather than sustained, static frontier defence.

Continued Barbarian pressure and a relaxation of T'ang offensive dynamism urged a change in military organisation by the middle of the 8th century. The status of militia service at the Imperial palace had declined in favour of specially raised elite units permanently entrusted to guarding the

Emperor. The praetorian tendency for such forces to be involved in palace intrigue was well understood by the Emperor Hsuan-tsung. In one attempted coup, the Northern Army guardsmen had to be put down by the Flying Dragon Palace Army, a corps under the direct command of the palace eunuchs. Increasingly, the Emperor cut the number of soldiers in his capital by sending them to the frontiers. One chronicler writes that Hsuan-tsung discouraged military preparation of any kind within the capital: 'The Emperor had spear and arrow points melted down in order to weaken his Imperial warriors. Anyone who carried warlike arms was punished and anyone who practised archery committed a crime. When worthless youths became soldiers their elders repudiated them and would not associate with them. Only in the frontier districts were large bodies of warriors maintained.'

On the frontier, the military situation was certainly different. Defence expenditure was stepped up by 50 per cent. By 737, no less than 85 per cent of the Empire's troops were under the control of regional military governors. Central government could not call upon a comparable force. In the same year, an edict ordered frontier troops to be permanently engaged in their region. Veterans were offered tax exemptions, land, and houses in order to settle on the frontier. No longer would seasoned troops be replaced by inexperienced militia recruits every three years. Military colonies of professional warriors were established on the frontiers and the militia ran down. The cost was high. Regional commanders demanded increased rewards if they were to bear the brunt of T'ang military policy. A greater degree of independence meant also that these military governors frequently added Barbarians to their forces. The rise of Barbarian officers within the provincial armies loosened their ties with central government. Loyalty resided with individual warlords, not with the Emperor. Had Hsuan-tsung's palace fears made the Empire vulnerable to an even greater danger?

It was on this wave of military change that An Lu-shan rode to high office. In 742, he became military governor of the P'ing-lu frontier district in the extreme north-east of the Empire. It was a peak position and entitled him to report regularly to the Emperor at the capital Ch'ang-an, in northern central China. It is said Lu-shan bribed government ministers to speak well of him at court to obtain advancement. This seems unnecessary. His military strength, political sense, and good humour made him a favourite at the Imperial palace. At this time, the Emperor was infatuated with a noted beauty, Yang Kuei-fei. She was installed in the Emperor's harem and adopted her name which means 'precious consort'. Once recognised as the Emperor's senior female confidant, she dominated the palace and became a key political figure. An Lu-shan enjoyed a close relationship with the consort. He bowed to her before doing homage to the Emperor. 'Why do you do this?' wondered Hsuan-tsung. 'My lord,' he replied, 'your subject is a mere Barbarian. A Barbarian puts his mother first and father afterwards.' In truth, Lu-shan realised the influence wielded by the beautiful woman.

Turkic painted stucco figure of a horse with decorated saddle. Naturally, An Lu-shan was an excellent rider. From Astana Cemetery in Xinjiang, north western China, late 6th to early 8th century.

53

Court gossip inevitably surrounded the warlord's friendship with Yang Kuei-fei. He had free access to the palace and spent many occasions in delicious debauchery in the harem. But between the warlord and the consort there appears to have been no impropriety. It was essentially an amusing friendship of mutual political advantage. Certainly the Emperor did not condemn it. He encouraged Lu-shan's advancement. In 744, he was awarded command of the Fan-yang frontier district next to P'ing-lu. In 750, he received a civil post in the Ho-pei province to the south of the Great Wall and the next year he added military governorship of the Ho-tung frontier district to his other two.

It was most unusual for one man to hold several governorships simultaneously, but the development was in line with the Emperor's wish to withdraw from active leadership and let the frontier look after itself. As the single most powerful man in north-east China, An Lu-shan set about consolidating his position there. In the north of Fan-yang, he built the fortress of Hsiung-wu. He declared it a key garrison against Barbarian bandits. Within it, he stored grain, livestock, weapons and 15,000 war horses. He attracted many important warrior chiefs to his standard and trained over 8,000 Tongra, Hsi, and Khitan warriors who had surrendered to him. To prove his loyalty to the Emperor, he sent a regular tribute of camels, horses, falcons, and dogs. He also demonstrated his fighting efficiency by sending bags of heads belonging to Khitan chieftains. But these were said to have been gained by deception rather than martial prowess. Khitan chieftains had been invited to join Lu-shan at a banquet. Their wine was drugged with the herb *scopolia japonica*. When the Khitan became intoxicated, their heads were struck off. 'None were aware of their deaths,' wrote the chronicler. Not all Lu-shan's assaults on the Barbarians were successful.

In 751, An Lu-shan led an army reputedly 50,000 strong against the Khitan. He was joined by Hsi horsemen. They rode north-eastwards beyond P'ing-lu to the land of the Khitan. The journey was long and the Hsi chieftain demanded a rest. Lu-shan's retainers assassinated him. The Hsi promptly deserted, warning the Khitan. Beyond the Lao river, the heartland of the Khitan, Lu-shan's army was ambushed. Heavy rain hampered the Chinese archery. Exhaustion lowered their strength. The Mongolian tribesmen surrounded them. An Lu-shan came under personal attack. An arrow shattered his jade hair-pin. He only just managed to escape back to P'ing-lu with the remnants of his army. Scapegoats were seized upon. Surviving subordinate officers were executed. Other more sensible commanders waited in the mountains for Lu-shan's anger to subside before reappearing.

In the capital, the Emperor had left policy-making completely to his chief minister, Li Lin-fu. Throughout the 740s and early 750s, Lin-fu acted as dictator. He fended off many conspiracies but in the end could not cheat death. In 752, his rivals emerged to battle for his position. Chief among

Painted earthenware figure of a tomb guardian, T'ang dynasty, early 8th century. The Imperial bodyguard of Hsuan-tsung wore similar, elaborate armour of decorated leather. Now in the British Museum, London.

Glazed earthenware model of a horse, early 8th century. In the T'ang dynasty, horses were used in greater force than ever before and celebrated in art. A reflection of the influence of steppe warfare on Chinese culture.

Glazed earthenware camel with dragon mouth saddle, T'ang dynasty, early 8th century. Camels were sent as tribute to the Emperor by central Asian chieftains. An Lu-shan probably incorporated camels into his army for carrying baggage.

these was Yang Kuo-chung, a cousin of Yang Kuei-fei. He assumed the title of Chief Minister and at once set about slandering the regime of Lin-fu. An Lu-shan would not accept these insults. He had no respect for the newcomer. Yang Kuo-chung did not trust the Barbarian warlord at all. He warned the Emperor that Lu-shan would rebel. Hsuan-tsung sent a eunuch to spy on the warlord. Lu-shan bribed the eunuch and he returned to the Emperor with glowing reports of his loyalty. Hsuan-tsung was assured of the warlord's allegiance and awarded him further Imperial posts, among them Commissioner of Horse Pastures, Stables, and Flocks. Lu-shan used the position to gather the finest animals for his warriors. If anyone advised the Emperor that An Lu-shan would rebel, Hsuan-tsung had them bound and sent to the warlord. In 755, this trust was ruptured.

Hsuan-tsung summoned An Lu-shan to his court. This time the warlord felt court politics were too dangerous. He said he was too ill to make the journey. The Emperor then presented a bride to Lu-shan's son and ordered him to attend the wedding. An Lu-shan refused. He had a strong military base. The 8,000 Barbarian soldiers he had trained formed the elite corps of an army said to number 100,000. The 8,000 were called 'sons', the most faithful of his warriors. Equipped with the finest horses and stock-piled weapons, Lu-shan decided the moment was right for his move. Before the government could mobilise forces against him, he ordered his warriors into the interior. He covered the raising of warriors by pretending to have received Imperial requests to counter a gang of bandits. In truth it was a rebellion against the Emperor and his Chief Minister. Travelling by night and eating at day-break, Lu-shan's Barbarian horde rode swiftly towards the capital. The cuts in the number of military garrisons in the interior meant the rebel army encountered little resistance.

In the winter of 755, An Lu-shan crossed the Yellow River. The ice would not hold his warriors so they hurled uprooted trees into the river to break it up. Their boats were pulled through the freezing waters and the next day the river froze again. An Lu-shan was in his early 50s and grotesquely fat. He had to be supported by two advisers when walking. On campaign he travelled in an iron palanquin. On top of his obesity, the warlord developed an irritating skin disease and his eyesight failed to the point that he could hardly see. The rigours of a winter campaign and the decay of his body made An Lu-shan intensely ill-tempered. He was quick to order execution and destruction. When he took a city, many of its inhabitants were slaughtered. Lu-shan had little interest in restraining the excesses of his Barbarian warriors. He simply urged them on to the capital with the promise of more plunder.

In January 756, the rebel army attacked the Imperial second capital of Lo-yang. The defenders burned the bridges leading to the city. They ripped down walls and trees in the Imperial gardens to build barricades. At the last moment, their nerve left them and they fled. Lu-shan angrily entered the ruined city. He proclaimed himself Emperor of a new dynasty: the Yen regime. He chose the title of 'Heroically Martial Emperor'. His Barbarian troops were jubilant. They were in the heart of an Empire that could become their own. An Lu-shan's coronation celebrations gave the Imperial army time to gather its forces. There were loyalist uprisings in areas under An Lu-shan's dominion. Weakening his rear guard, it prevented advance westwards. As he remained in Lo-yang, Imperial forces drew a line of defence at T'ung-kuan Pass on the road to the capital. The two armies faced each other in a stalemate.

An Lu-shan was reluctant to attack. The arrival of fresh Imperial troops in his old regions stiffened the loyalist revolts. Valuable P'ing-lu frontier units broke away and joined the Imperial army. Suddenly, Lu-shan's conquests seemed to be disappearing from behind him. To Yang Kuo-chung at the Imperial court in the capital, the opportunity seemed right for a major counterattack to clear the rebel army at T'ung-kuan Pass. A massive army of 80,000 horsemen and footsoldiers assembled. In July, the Imperial army attacked the rebels west of Ling-pao. The details of the battle are vague, but the confrontation of two major Chinese armies must have been a spectacle. The high proportion of Turkic and Mongolian horse-warriors on both sides ensured a monumental cavalry battle. Whistling arrows were shot high in the air, opening the combat. Horse-archers dashed forward on their steppe ponies, the smooth drumming canter of these small animals being ideal for the shooting of composite bows. Catching the bamboo shafts and steel tips on their mail and leather armour, the more heavily armed horsemen awaited the attack.

Armour was highly valued by the Chinese. To prevent it reaching the Barbarians, the Chinese punished the unauthorised transport and possession of armour and weapons with long prison sentences and exile. But An Lu-shan had purposely gathered the finest arms for his followers. Old forms of armour made from the leather of wild animals, including rhinoceros, buffalo, and shark, were widely available. Metal plate from Korea and scale armour from Tibet were accompanied by mail, recently introduced into China from central Asia. In the battle for the T'ung-kuan Pass, the heavily armoured cavalry of both sides weathered the arrow storm. Contingents of footsoldiers ventured onto the battlefield possessing crossbows and long bladed polearms, but on the whole they were restricted to guarding the baggage trains and forming a rear guard. Once the light cavalry had exhausted themselves and exploitable gaps could be observed, the first units of heavily armoured horsemen thundered forward. They rode bigger, handsome Arab chargers. As warriors clashed and broke, sabres and single-edged daggers were unsheathed. With slashing and cutting the battle would be determined. The Imperial commanders needed a victory. They sent in the Imperial Guard. Magnificently clad in embroidered leather breastplates, shoulder pads, tassets, and greaves, they were the elite forces. It was not enough. The Barbarians were far from overawed. They held and smashed the Imperial resolve. The Imperial army was completely defeated.

Turkic warrior in scale
armour. Many such
horsemen rode in An Lu-
shan's army. From Ming-
oi, north west China, 8th
century, now in the
British Museum, London.

A. WARRIOR IN SCALE ARMOUR
MINGOI. c. 8TH - 10TH CENTURY.
"Serindia". Plate CXXXV. Mi.xii. 0010, 0015, 0017.

It fled to the capital, leaving the T'ung-kuan Pass wide open.

The Emperor was advised to evacuate the capital. On the way south-west to safety, demoralised and defeated Imperial soldiers seized the caravan of Yang Kuo-chung. He was dragged from his wagon and killed. The soldiers then demanded the execution of the Emperor's favourite. Reluctantly, the Emperor consented to the strangling of Yang Kuei-fei in order to save his own life. The Heir Apparent, Su-tsung, gathered all remaining Imperial troops and made for the north-west frontier. A few days

Earthenware figure of a rider and horse clad in cloth or leather armour. An Lu-shan's heavy cavalry probably wore similar protection against the archery of their adversaries. Six Dynasties Period, 7th century.

later he proclaimed himself Emperor. With the capital deserted, rebel warriors entered Ch'ang-an. Two Imperialist assaults on the capital were beaten off. The loyalist rebellion in P'ing-lu was finally subdued. An Lu-shan was at the peak of his career. But the warlord was suffering. His skin disease and blindness enraged him. He treated his officers harshly, dismembering anyone found guilty of even minor crimes with axes and halberds. In this atmosphere, Lu-shan's subordinates began to doubt the longevity of their lord as an effective leader. Loyalty had turned to fear. Conspiracy grew.

Yen Chuang, one of Lu-shan's foremost advisers, was flogged. He spoke to his master's principal heir, An Ch'ung-hsu. The two agreed Lu-shan could no longer lead them. On the evening of 29 January 757, An Ch'ung-hsu stood outside the door to his father's tent in Lo-yang. Chuang entered with a Khitan eunuch called Li Chu-erh. As Lu-shan lay dozing, Chu-erh pierced his massive bulk with a sword. Many years ago, it had been Lu-shan who had severed Chu-erh's sexual organs and made him a eunuch. Lu-shan had favoured Chu-erh greatly, allowing him the intimacy of dressing him, lifting his great stomach to secure his loose clothes. Now, the eunuch aimed all his frustration at the belly of the blind warlord. Lu-shan awoke. He groped for the sword that always lay at the head of his bed. It was gone. He grabbed the curtains around his bed and cried: 'There is a thief in my house.' The eunuch plunged the blade again and again into Lu-shan's thick stomach. Finally the warlord's words ceased. Chuang ordered the huge carcass wrapped in a carpet. A hole was dug beneath Lu-shan's bed and the corpse rolled into it. Outside the tent, Chuang announced that Lu-shan had died suddenly from his illness and Ch'ung-hsu was the new rebel leader.

The rebellion begun by An Lu-shan did not end with his death. A desperate guerrilla war waged back and forth for six more years. An Ch'ung-hsu proved an incompetent commander. Within months, the Emperor Su-tsung had re-captured the capital with the help of 3,000 Uighur Turkic tribesmen. Lo-yang soon after fell and the rebels fell back to Ho-pei. There, Ch'ung-hsu was deposed from his leadership and condemned for the murder of his father. He was strangled. Eventually, Imperial forces triumphed in 763. But such was the state of the country that the T'ang dynasty could no longer exert absolute control over its provinces. The action of An Lu-shan had shattered the ancient unity of China and introduced the country to the power and devastation of the warlord. To the Barbarian warriors on the north-east frontier, he became a cult figure – the realisation of all their ambitions.

OWEN OF WALES

Before the King of France, Owen explained himself. He claimed he was the grandson of a Celtic prince of Wales. King Edward I of England had conquered Wales, and slain Owen's grandfather along with his brother, Llywelyn, the last true ruler of Wales. All Owen's inheritance had been given to Edward's son, falsely named Prince of Wales, a mere puppet of English tyranny. Owen's father was the next to suffer. Slaughtered by the English King, he too had all his land taken. Owen fled from the English simply to save his life. Would the great and just King of France accept Owen into his service so he could one day avenge his family and claim his estates in Wales? The King was uncertain. Many adventurers came to his court, boasting of an illustrious background now lost, and seeking lucrative employment. Was this mysterious Welsh warrior speaking the truth?

Ever since Owen appeared at the court of Philip VI of France, historians have tried to prove the Welshman's royal lineage. Among those who have traced his career, respect is high. 'He is probably the greatest military genius that Wales has produced,' enthuses one historian, while a near contemporary chronicler claims that Owain Glyndwr was inspired by the exploits of his earlier namesake. From what little evidence remains, it seems that Owen was in fact the grandson of Rhodri ap Gruffydd, brother of Llywelyn. But far from being a valiant Celtic supporter of the last Welsh prince of Wales, documents reveal that Rhodri had been settled upon an English estate by Edward I and was quite happy to serve the English King. In 1278, Rhodri entered into a bitter dispute with his brother

The usurper John is brought for execution before the Western Imperial regent Placidia, and her *bucellarii*. Aquileia, north east Italy, 425 AD.

Alan horseman of Orleans, on the orders of Aetius, clashes with *bacaudae* on an estate in eastern Brittany, 440s.

The Warlord Aetius and a Burgundian retainer attacked by a Hun at the battle of *locus Mauriacus*, north west France, 451.

Vandal and Moorish pirates flee to their ship after an ambush set by *bucellarii* of the Western Emperor Majorian. Campania, south west Italy, c.458.

Gaiseric's Moorish warriors in a camel phalanx attacked by Huns in the Eastern Imperial warlord Heraclius's army. Tripolis, North Africa, 468.

An Lu-shan pursues a Khitan Mongol beyond the Great Wall on the north-east Chinese border, 735.

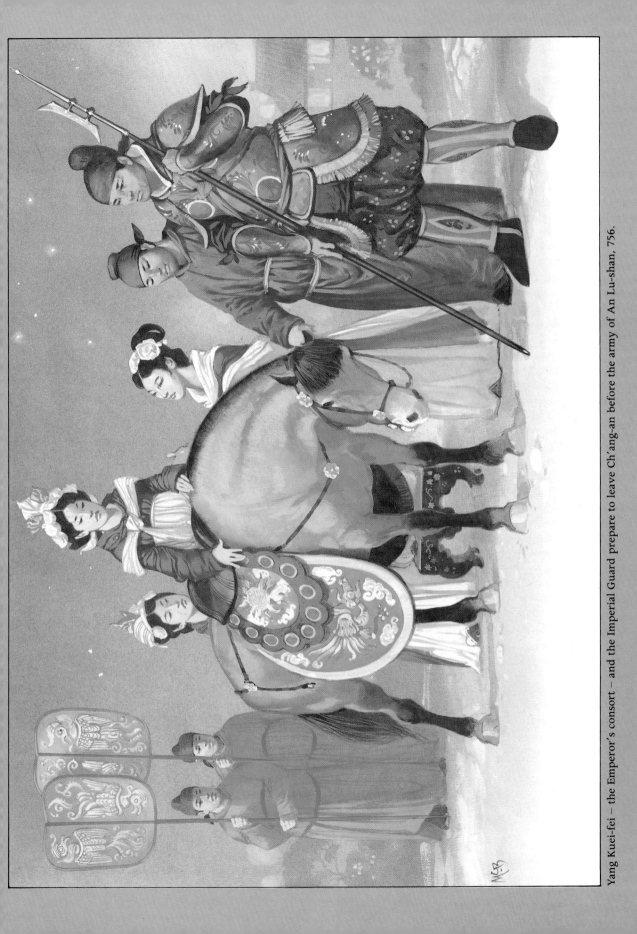

Yang Kuei-fei – the Emperor's consort – and the Imperial Guard prepare to leave Ch'ang-an before the army of An Lu-shan, 756.

Spanish galley collides with English cog at the battle of Rochelle, French coast, 1372.

Owen of Wales is pursued by halberdiers from Berne at Buttisholz, Switzerland, 1375.

Bertrand du Guesclin and his retainers surprise men-at-arms of Sir Hugh Calverly on the road to Montmuran, Brittany, 1354.

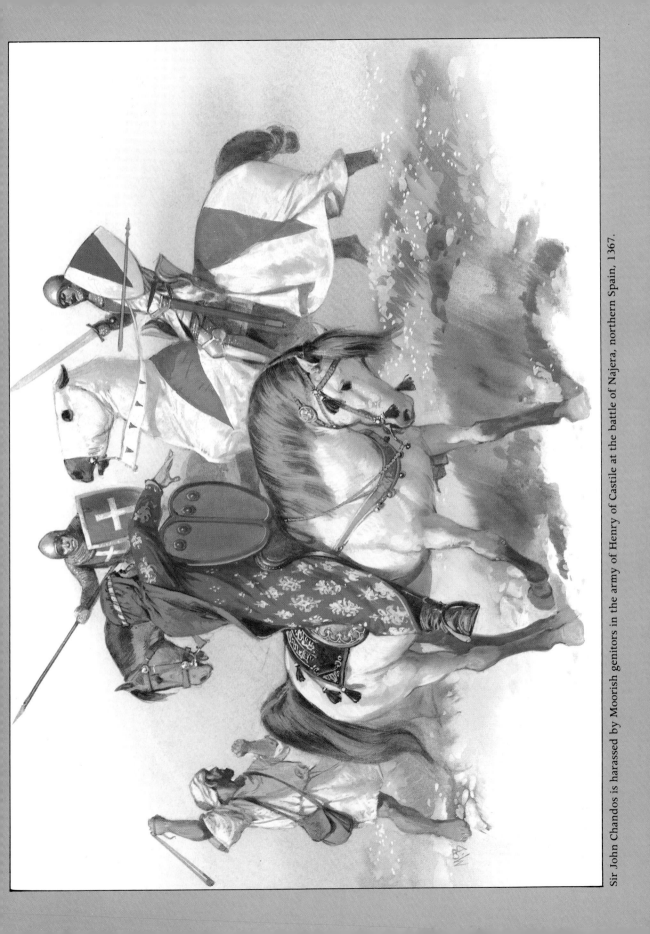

Sir John Chandos is harassed by Moorish genitors in the army of Henry of Castile at the battle of Nájera, northern Spain, 1367.

Teutonic knight attacked by Lithuanian horse-archers at the battle of Tannenberg, 1410.

Taborite war wagons await the attack of Sigismund's Hungarian horsemen. Outside Kutna Hora, 1421, eastern Bohemia.

Jan Zizka enters Prague with his Orebite warriors, 1423.

Dracula supervises the execution of prisoners after a raid on a German settlement in southern Transylvania, 1460.

Wallachian horsemen surprise janissaries crossing the Danube, southern Romanian border, 1462.

Llywelyn. In an English court, Rhodri argued that land belonging to his uncle in north Wales was being withheld by Llywelyn. Eventually, it was agreed that Rhodri should forgo his claims to the Welsh land and settle for 950 marks paid by Llywelyn. In 1282, Llywelyn was killed by the English. Rhodri lived on comfortably in England receiving a pension from the English treasury.

The only son of Rhodri's second wife was called Thomas. He lived as an English gentlemen on his Tatsfield estate in Surrey. He sold family land in Cheshire and bought a small manor in Gloucester. Like his father, Thomas was always keen to exploit his Welsh connection in the pursuit of land. He bought a small estate in north Wales and made an unsuccessful attempt to claim some of the patrimony of his ancestors. Thomas bought the Welsh manor of Dinas from John de Cherleton in 1333. Cherleton was an active knight in the King's service in Ireland. Relations between Cherleton and Thomas were not good. Five years later, Cherleton and his retainers seized Dinas. Thomas sought redress through the courts and received money from Cherleton but not his manor. Thomas spent the remainder of his life on his English estates. This is the true background of Owen, son of Thomas, son of Rhodri. His family had a history of collaboration with the English. They sought conflict only through the courts. Neither his father nor his grandfather died violently at the hands of the Edwardian conquerors.

At the age of 20 Owen stood before Philip VI and elaborated his life. The French King was impressed by his hatred of the English. Whatever his true background, Philip employed the imaginative Welshman at his court. In time, Owen became a favourite of the Valois court and after the death of Philip, in 1350, he continued to serve under King John. In 1356, Owen fought on the French side at the battle of Poitiers. The combat was a disaster. The French army was shattered and King John captured. French fortunes could not have been lower. A humiliating treaty in 1360 ensured English presence in France. There was continued raiding throughout the country and civil war in Brittany. Owen saw no reason to remain in France. He had lost his patron. With a group of adventuring knights, he rode into northern Italy seeking employment.

Owen's father died in 1363. The news took time to reach Owen. He had been away from England for many years and probably no longer considered it his home. His relationship with his father appears not to have been close and may account for his fantasy background. Certainly, the officials dealing with the disposal of Thomas' estate knew of no heir. Sometime in 1365, Owen appeared in England. Just like his forefathers, he sought justice through the court of the King of England. He was successful, obtaining both Dinas and his English estates with few problems. But retirement on a minor landholding in an alien country did not suit Owen. He continued with his fictional tales of woe. He left England and travelled to several European courts. Each time, the story of his lost inheritance became more tragic. He began to conceive of himself as the rightful heir to the entire principality of

Wales. Welsh retainers in his company fuelled the fantasy and encouraged his story-telling before European monarchs.

War broke out again between France and England in 1369. Owen presented himself to the new King of France, Charles V. He was placed in charge of a fleet and several thousand soldiers at the port of Harfleur. Charles was excited by the prospect of a sea-war against the English. A treaty allowed him to call upon the powerful Spanish fleet of King Henry of Castile. In the spring of 1372, Spanish and French naval strength was demonstrated before the port of Rochelle. The town was besieged by the French and the English hoped to relieve it. An English fleet under the command of the Earl of Pembroke sailed from Southampton. His navy included big, deep draught ships with single square sails and stern rudders. These were a medieval innovation, called cogs. Clinker-built galleys, powered by 100 oars, and with an oar-shaped rudder hanging over the side, were still common in northern waters. In addition to these fighting ships were smaller oar-driven barges mainly used for the transportation of troops.

As the English sailed into view of Rochelle, they sighted a large Spanish fleet of over 50 sailing ships and galleys blocking their way. The English were outnumbered, but committed to the relief of Rochelle. Battle stations were ordered. Archers assembled in the wooden castles on the bows. The Spanish ships were bigger than the English, with taller towers and ramparts. While the English prepared for the clash, the Spanish took the offensive. They caught the wind and bore down hard full sail. The castles of their ships were crammed with cannon and armoured soldiers shooting crossbows and handguns. The noise was terrific. Stone and iron cannonballs crashed through the English planking. The Spanish craft closed in. From their higher decks, iron and lead bars were flung down, ripping great holes in the hulls of the English cogs and galleys. A hail of bolts and arrows swept the decks.

67

Despite the inferior size of their ships, the English put up a brave fight. Their spears tipped Spanish men-at-arms into the waves. All the time, they expected the English garrison at Rochelle to sail out and join the battle. The English knights within the castle of Rochelle were indeed trying to raise assistance from the townsmen to reinforce their comrades. But the townsmen were essentially French and had little sympathy for the English cause. The battle in the harbour came to an end with nightfall. Aside from numerous casualties, the English had had two barges sunk containing provisions. The next day, the Spanish weighed anchor and resumed battle order. Under a blast of trumpets, drums, and cannon, the Spanish ships formed a line, hoping to surround the English huddled together. But the English too broke open into a line, placing their archers in barges as a vanguard. The Spanish sailed close to the English. They flung grappling hooks with chains of iron, lashing themselves to the English in fierce hand-to-hand combat. Again, the larger, higher vessels had the advantage. Iron and lead bars smashed the wooden structures. Several prominent English knights were slain. Their ships were boarded. The Earl of Pembroke was captured. With great victory and booty to match, the Spaniards set sail and left Rochelle to the French.

Whether Owen was present at this battle, or just viewed it from the shore, its outcome greatly influenced his life. Charles V committed him to a career of seamanship. In May 1372, from the port of Harfleur, Owen issued a proclamation of thanks and debt to the King of France. He began his declaration with an account of his royal Welsh lineage, the slaughter and exile of his family, and the claim that Wales was his by right of descent. He then thanked Charles for recognising his plight and providing funds for the restoration of his inheritance. He had received 300,000 francs of gold and command of 4,000 men-at-arms, archers, crossbowmen, and sailors. He promised to repay the sum in his own lifetime or through his successors. Finally, he ensured an alliance between France and his own country, Wales. In this declaration, he styled himself Yvan de Galles: Owen of Wales. This is the name by which the French knew him throughout his campaigns against the English.

In the summer of 1372, Owen's French fleet sailed from Harfleur. His declaration of May suggests it was an invasion fleet intent on reaching Wales. Whether by design or chance, it actually landed on the coast of the island of Guernsey, not far off the coast of Normandy. Edmund Rose was captain of the English garrison at Guernsey. An alarm resounded throughout the island and 800 men gathered. Somewhere near St Peter Port, the English and French clashed. It was a savage encounter. Over 400 Englishmen are said to have been slain. Rose's army broke, making for Castle Cornet on an island in the harbour of St Peter Port. Owen rallied his men and tried to take the castle by assault. The castle was strong and well provided with weapons and cannon. Owen settled for a siege.

After the battle of Rochelle, the Spanish fleet had returned to Castile. But

Seal of the port of Poole,
1325, illustrating a typical
English clinker-built cog
with single sail, rear
rudder and castles.

69

Charles V was so highly pleased with their performance that he wanted to continue the seaborne campaign against the English. Hearing that Owen was bogged down on the island of Guernsey, he ordered the Welshman to forget the siege and sail to Spain. There, he was to invite the King of Castile, his admiral, and all available ships to lay siege to Rochelle and finally take the stubborn English castle. Contrary winds had slowed the return of the Spanish fleet and Owen caught up with them along the coast of Galicia in north-west Spain. At the port of Santander, the Spaniards disembarked. Their prisoners were taken in chains to the port's castle. Owen was told of the presence of the Earl of Pembroke among them. He made for the chamber in which Pembroke was held. He had never met the Welsh Earl before. Pembroke was surprised to hear an English voice.

'Who are you, that you speak my language?'

'I am Owen, son of a true prince of Wales, whom your King put to death and disinherited. But with the help of my dear lord, the King of France, I shall remedy that. Let it be known that if I ever cross you again I shall fight you and reveal the wrong you have done me and my father.'

At this, one of Pembroke's knights stepped forward.

'Owen, if any wrong has been done to you by my lord, and if you maintain he should do homage to you or any of your ancestors, throw down your gauntlet. I shall pick it up.'

'You are a prisoner,' replied Owen. 'No honour can be won from you. When you are free, we shall talk about this matter, for it cannot rest.'

The English knight angrily dragged his chains forward. Spanish knights intervened and separated Owen from his challenger.

Aside from his impotent meeting with Pembroke, Owen's mission to Spain was a complete success. He arrived before Rochelle with the Spanish admiral, Don Ruy Diaz de Rojas, 40 great ships, and 8 galleys full of soldiers. The fleet blockaded the port. The civilian townsmen of Rochelle sent envoys to Owen and the Spanish admiral agreeing not to assist the English garrison so long as the fleet left them alone. The secret truce was accepted. Owen sent scouts into the surrounding countryside to gather information. In the meanwhile, the Constable of France, Bertrand du Guesclin, had sent 300 lances under the Lord of Pons to capture the nearby castle of Soubise. At the mouth of the river Charente, it was only a few miles from Rochelle. The Lady of the castle had few warriors and sent for help from Jean de Grailly, commander of English forces in Aquitaine. Owen also realised the strategic value of this river-mouth castle. All three forces converged on Soubise.

Owen decided on an approach by sea. He filled three barges with 400 men. Neither the French Lord of Pons nor Jean de Grailly knew of Owen's presence. Grailly expected little conflict and reduced his force by 100 lances. At night, he surprised the French in a fierce skirmish. The Lord of Pons and 60 men-at-arms were captured. Owen heard the struggle. He ordered his men to light torches and plunged into the dark. With 400 men, he descended upon the English and Gascon warriors. Grailly had thought

victory was his and allowed his men to split up in pursuit of booty and prisoners. They were easily overcome. By the light of the flaming torches, an English knight recognised Owen and called him a traitor to the King of England. Owen struck him down with his battle-axe. The next day, the rescued Lord of Pons joined Owen in an assault upon Soubise. The Lady of the castle resisted strongly but in the end admitted defeat.

As town after town fell to the French, Rochelle became isolated. Its townsmen were keen for the siege to end, but could do nothing while their castle remained in English hands. The Town Mayor, Jean Caudourier, assembled those sympathetic to the French and suggested a plan. He told them that Philip Mansell, the English captain of the castle, was not a man of great intelligence. He proposed to pretend to receive an order from the King of England commanding the assessment of all armed men in Rochelle. Over dinner, he told Mansell of the letter. A manuscript bearing King Edward's seal was shown to the captain. The words referred to a matter many months old, but Mansell could not read. The Mayor had the desired meaning read out. All the townsmen were to be armed and assembled before the castle. Likewise, Mansell's garrison was to parade outside the walls. The Mayor could then assure King Edward of Rochelle's ability to resist the French. He added also that the King commanded him to pay the garrison out of his own funds. Mansell agreed.

The next morning, the Mayor assembled 2,000 men near the castle wall. The watch bell sounded and Mansell proceeded across the drawbridge with 60 men-at-arms. As they assembled keenly before the Mayor, awaiting their pay, the townsmen surrounded them. Thus the port of Rochelle fell into French hands. Out in the bay, Owen heard he was not to be allowed the honour of entering the town. The people of Rochelle carried out careful negotiations with the French King before opening their gates to any troops. In the end, the port pledged its loyalty in return for permission to mint its own coins. It was left to Bertrand du Guesclin to receive the official welcome and homage of the townsmen.

After Rochelle, Owen joined the company of Bertrand du Guesclin. He became involved in the civil war in Brittany. But he also retained his reputation as a powerful naval commander with Spanish connections. In 1373, the King of England feared Owen was planning an invasion with 6,000 men. An English fleet of 60 ships and 2,000 men-at-arms sailed from Cornwall to confront it. Nothing happened, but it appears Owen was still very much in control of French coastal waters, indulging in profitable piracy and raiding. In 1375, a year's truce was declared. To maintain his income and keep his followers together, Owen sought service with mercenary companies in Switzerland. The Hapsburgs frequently sent punitive expeditions against the rebellious Swiss cantons. In December, Owen and his Austrian commander were confronted by Swiss troops at Buttisholz. Pike and halberd phalanxes from Lucerne, Entelbuch, and Unterwalden repulsed the mercenary horsemen. The Swiss were angry at

their persistent looting and destruction. Other Swiss soldiers from Berne and Fribourg pursued the foreign companies, inflicting two more defeats on them. It must have been with great relief that Owen heard of the resumption of hostilities in France.

14th century helmet adapted with iron handle and chain to suspend over a fire as a cooking-pot. Found in Southwark, London, now in the British Museum.

In 1377, Owen was employed alongside Bertrand du Guesclin by the Duke of Anjou on a campaign against Gascony, a region sympathetic to England. They laid siege to the town of Bergerac. Skirmishing outside the walls proved indecisive and the Duke sent for a war engine: a massive device that cast rocks and carried 100 men within it towards the wall. Apparently, the pieces for the machine could only be obtained from the nearby town of La Reole. 300 French lances rode out. Information was then received of a sighting of 400 English lances from Bordeaux in the vicinity. A rearguard of 200 lances, including Owen, was sent after the Frenchmen. All three forces met near Ymet. The skirmish was fought on horseback with lances couched. Froissart described the initial encounter as a joust. But then a French squire was struck in the throat, slicing his jugular vein. Several more knights died. When their lances were broken, swords were drawn. Finally, the French were triumphant. The sight of the great siege engine outside Bergerac soon convinced the town to yield. Owen's part in this campaign reveals that though he might be a notorious privateer, on land he was a minor warlord and still expected to fight in the field.

Throughout the summer of 1377, the Duke of Anjou took a succession of Gascon towns. Eventually he tired and wished to return home to Toulouse. He garrisoned his conquests and ordered his followers to continue the campaign. Owen was given 500 lances of Bretons, Angevins, and other Frenchmen. He must lay siege to the castle of Mortaigne, at the mouth of the river Garonne. He must not leave the siege for any other lord, not even the King, until he had taken it. Owen agreed. He knew that whatever the Duke ordered had the permission of the King and his funding. A great many notable knights rode under his command. Owen was now regarded as an independent warlord. Perhaps his earlier action at Bergerac impressed the Duke.

At Mortaigne, Owen ordered the digging of earthworks to cut it off from sea and land. It was a strong castle and Owen did not favour an assault. As the wood and earth barricades were erected around the castle, young knights of both sides skirmished with each other. It was the only chance they had to achieve feats of arms. The grim, slow business of siege was too dull for these young men, offering them no opportunity to display their martial skills and win personal advancement. As the knights passed the time in deadly jousts, news came through of the death of Edward III. It made little difference. The siege dragged on for 18 months. The war continued. In Bordeaux, the English commanders were becoming tired of the gradual reduction of their possessions. Town after town, castle after castle fell under French dominion. Plans were devised to halt the French advance. A hit-list of primary French warlords was drawn up.

A Welshman called John Lamb joined Owen's camp at Mortaigne sometime in 1378. This was nothing unusual. Owen always had a warm welcome for Celtic exiles. He loved to hear the language of his forefathers and news of Wales. Lamb spoke Welsh fluently and eagerly, telling Owen that his reputation was high among his countrymen. They all desired the warlord to return and lead the Welsh against the English. Owen was overjoyed to hear these words and made Lamb his personal servant. Every morning, Owen sat before the castle of Mortaigne and prepared himself for the day. Lamb accompanied him, combing his hair. One such morning, it had been a hot night and Owen rose early. As everyone slept, he proceeded to sit before the fortress and ponder his fate. He felt confident the castle would soon fall. He asked Lamb to fetch his comb. Lamb went away and returned with a comb. In addition, he carried a short Spanish javelin with a long blade of steel. As Owen sat on the grass, Lamb plunged the spear into his master's back. Owen rolled forward. Lamb left the spear in the body and quickly departed, making his way through the earthworks and entering the castle.

The captain of Mortaigne, the Lord Letrau, was far from pleased. Although desperate, he knew a code existed between knights in which their mutual safe-keeping was assured whatever happened to them. Captured knights were always well treated. The murder of a great knight such as Owen by a treacherous nobody like Lamb would not reflect well on Letrau's chivalric reputation. These things mattered. 'We shall have blame rather than praise for this,' he concluded. Besides, Owen's army would be angry and likely to order the assault of the castle with no quarter given. In Owen's camp, there was much grieving. His body was carried to the graveyard of the local church of Saint Leger and buried near one of the earthworks he had erected. All the noble knights swore to avenge his death and take the castle at once. This was not to be.

Falchion of the mid 14th century, a heavy slashing sword.

A large force of English and Gascon troops sailed down the river Garonne to relieve Mortaigne. Despite the great investment of time and their vows, the majority of French knights quickly withdrew. Only Owen's closest Breton and Welsh retainers would not give up so easily. They gathered all their weapons and missiles into the church of Saint Leger. Within sight of their dead lord, they made their last stand. The English arrived in barges. Men-at-arms with crossbows crept up on the church. A fierce skirmish lasted for three hours. The church was built upon a great rock and not easily approached. With many men hurt, the English retreated. Owen's followers spent the night with Saint Leger. At daybreak the English knights ordered a major assault. Trumpets were sounded and the English advanced. Arrows and crossbow bolts shattered the stained-glass windows. Owen's followers huddled among the pews and before the altar. Chunks of decoration fell to the floor beneath the barrage. Plaster and wood splintered. The English battered against the substantial church doors. The French retaliated. The English were beaten back. The siege earthworks were proving the greatest obstacle to a clear attack. The English began to fill in the ditches and tear down the barricades. As the Bretons and Welsh observed the magnitude of the forces gathering against them, their nerve finally left them. Heralds were sent out and a truce accepted. The followers of Owen were granted safe passage out of Saint Leger on account of their defence of their dead lord's honour.

Despite the lord of Mortaigne's chilvaric conceit, the English were highly pleased with Owen's assassination. Lamb received a payment of £20 from the court in England and a sum of 522 livres 10 sous from the English government in Bordeaux. Charles V was greatly saddened by Owen's death. The war was far from won. He needed more such warlords to support the efforts of Bertrand du Guesclin. The Welsh missed him too. Although they never knew his rule and Owen's claims to Welsh leadership were laced with fantasy, the humbled principality was happy to celebrate any hero of Welsh blood. Even better if that man was a notorious batterer of the English. Welsh poets created myths around his life. He was called Owen Lawgoch: Owen of the Red Hand, or Owen the Outlaw. He was not dead in France. They believed he slept with his followers in a cave in south Wales awaiting the bell of destiny to lead him forth to conquer the English and win back the land of his forefathers. In Welsh minds, Owen became another Arthur.

BERTRAND DU GUESCLIN

'Perceval was a huntsman,' recalled the poet. 'He rode into the forest with his javelins. As he practised the throwing of spears, he heard a clattering of wood against iron. Perceval was frightened. His mother had told him that devils make the most terrible noise. He crossed himself and gripped his javelins. Out of the wood came the most beautiful sight. Figures wearing sparkling metal clothing, carrying long spears with red and green banners, rounded pieces of metal bearing gold and silver.

'My God, these are not devils,' said Perceval, 'but angels.' Before the beautiful creatures, he threw himself upon the ground. One of the figures rode forward.

'Be not afraid, young man,' he said.

'But you are angels?'

'No, we are knights.'

The adolescent Bertrand du Guesclin listened with wonder. Beyond the walls of La Motte-Broons, he imagined the encounter in the thick Celtic forest of Brittany. An awkward forestboy, wishing above all else to be a knight, Bertrand knew this was the only way for him to transcend his unhappy circumstances. By all accounts, he was an ugly, violent boy: disliked even by his parents. He could not count upon friendship or good looks to win him respect. But fighting would. He had little fear of physical violence or pain. When not the victim of beatings, he beat the young aristocrats and servants around him. At one time, he had to be locked in his father's dungeon. He was a bully and a thug. The warlord had already emerged.

At the age of around 21 in 1341, Bertrand du Guesclin was a muscular, stocky young man. In his presence, other men felt anxious: intimidated by his fearless pursuit of physical action. He wrestled as well as he jousted. He was a warrior in need of a war. In that same year, French politics provided it. John, Duke of Brittany, died without children. His niece, Jeanne de Penthièvre, was married to Charles, Count of Blois, nephew of Philip of Valois, the King of France. Valois saw at last an opportunity to bring the semi-independent Duchy of Brittany closer to his crown. But Valois and Blois were blocked by another claimant, the Count of Montfort, half brother of the dead Duke. Montfort acted quickly and seized both Rennes and Nantes, the chief cities of the Duchy. He proclaimed himself Duke of Brittany. Valois took Montfort to court and transferred the title to Blois. Montfort escaped back to Brittany and called upon Edward III, King of England, to assist him. Edward had already claimed the crown of France and so civil war in Brittany merged into the opening rounds of the Hundred Years War. Bertrand du Guesclin and his Breton family favoured the cause of the Count of Blois and the French King.

The fighting in Brittany was typical of medieval warfare: bands of marauders surprising each other in short-lived skirmishes. Such warfare could and would last for years. It was an environment of relentless hostility in which Guesclin thrived. He learned his trade in the forests of Brittany and built up a reputation as a man who succeeded in whichever way was required. In 1350, he disguised 60 of his followers as wood-cutters. They burst into the castle of Fougeray while its English commander was away plundering. As the English returned, Guesclin ambushed them. In the skirmishing that followed, Guesclin captured the nobleman Baron de la Poole. The English knight bore the insignia of a hen, so ever after Guesclin joked that the Breton eagle – the black two-headed eagle on his shield – had plucked the English hen.

In 1354, another demonstration of Guesclin's early military prowess was recorded. The English had occupied several towns in Brittany and Sir Hugh Calverly wished to capture the castle of Montmuran. Knights did not receive a regular wage from their commanders and had to pursue their own raiding campaigns to ensure an income and a following. The Lady of Montmuran had organised a grand banquet for several leading French warlords. Word reached her of the advancing English. Guesclin, one of her lesser guests, at once led forth 30 mounted archers and placed himself along the trail travelled by Calverly. As the English raiders rode past, Guesclin sprang his ambush and cut them down, carefully preserving Calverly however for profitable ransom. For this action Guesclin was knighted. The ambush is characteristic of the small-scale raid and counter-raid that constituted much of the Hundred Years War. It was such guerrilla conflict that made war economically viable.

In 1346 and 1356 at the battles of Crecy and Poitiers, the French forces of Philip and then John, Kings of France, were devastated. These famous

English victories have long been ascribed to the power of their archers. Over the centuries, the English longbowman has been heroised. Through association with these triumphs, his bow has been regarded as the supreme missile weapon of the Middle Ages. In reality, the so-called English longbow was a very ordinary weapon of no great power, considerably inferior to other contemporary continental bows of a more sophisticated design as well as the much maligned crossbow.

To begin with, the word 'longbow' did not exist in medieval vocabulary, it was simply called a bow. What is today identified as a 'longbow' is based in design upon the Victorian sporting bow which received its legendary name from manufacturers who saw it as a good selling point. The typical 14th century English bow, as far as it can be reconstructed, was a simple, thick, often inefficient wooden weapon. Bow design on the continent was far more sophisticated. Lighter, reflexed, composite bows were available. Superior to all, was the crossbow: the most powerful missile weapon in western Europe. Often made with a composite bow of sinew, wood, and horn, it could hurl a bolt 300 yards and further, beyond an average range of 200 yards for the 'longbow'. At this long range, the crossbow was not shouldered to aim, but held at a 45 degree angle so as to deliver its steel-tipped bolts as an artillery barrage. As for the much repeated criticism that it was slow to use, practical research and medieval illustrations reveal the rapid way to shoot crossbows.

In the illuminated manuscript of Froissart's Chronicles in the Bibliotheque Nationale, Paris, one crossbowman is depicted loading his weapon, while another shoots his. Historians have assumed that each bowman was in charge of both loading and shooting his own weapon. But one of the crossbowmen in the painting wears a box of quarrels around his waist and the other does not. From practical research, it is possible for two men to shoot two crossbows in rapid succession if one man specialises in drawing the strings of the bows and then hands them to a shooter who concentrates on aiming them. Thus a team of two men can keep up a hail of crossbow bolts long after the muscle fatigue of the solitary 'longbowman' has begun to slow his rate of shooting. At Jaffa, during the Third Crusade, it is recorded that Richard I's crossbowmen were employed in pairs: one to load, one to shoot.

The outcome of both Poitiers and Crecy was not due to the superior bows and bowmanship of the English, but a host of other reasons: principally, French incompetence. The most effective aspect of the English archers was that they were organised in massed formations in strong defensive positions, thus delivering an artillery shock to the French who had allowed themselves to be provoked into attacking at a disadvantage. These truths Bertrand du Guesclin knew. His warrior brigands were armed with both fine reflexed bows and crossbows. The individual English archer held no fear for him. It was the folly of confronting massed archers in strong defensive positions that he wished to avoid.

In his freelance guerrilla war in Brittany, Guesclin had become master of his own swift-moving retinue. In 1356, the Duke of Lancaster, in support of the Montfort claim, besieged Rennes. Guesclin maintained the pressure on the English through a series of raids on the area, but Lancaster was resolved to take the city. 'By the blood of Christ and by the Virgin His Mother,' he had sworn, 'I will not raise the siege until I have placed my banner on those walls.' In response, Guesclin became bolder. He attacked the English camp. Lancaster tried to speed up the siege. He ordered sappers to undermine the city walls. To discover the routes of these mines, the ever-resourceful citizens of Rennes hung copper pots with lead balls in the cellars nearest the walls. When the vibrations of the subterranean attackers shook the balls in the pots, the citizens knew they were underneath. Counter-mines were dug and noxious, smoking materials flung down at the English sappers. But ingenuity could not feed stomachs. Famine threatened to achieve what Lancaster could not.

Charles of Blois directed two armies to the relief of Rennes. One was defeated by Lancaster, but the other, commanded by Thibaud de Rochefort, made for Dinan. There he was joined by Guesclin. The two continued to ravage the English. Lancaster assaulted Dinan. He failed, but Guesclin realised the garrison could not hold out for long and agreed upon a truce. If, at the end of the truce, Dinan had not been relieved, then it would surrender. As Guesclin waited, his brother was captured by an English knight, Thomas of Canterbury. Guesclin was outraged at the violation of the truce. He rode to Lancaster's camp. Guesclin stated the trangression and the English knights agreed that honour should be satisfied. A combat was arranged in Dinan between Guesclin and Canterbury. The English knight John Chandos lent Guesclin his own horse and armour as the Breton's equipment was not fine enough for such a contest.

On the day of the duel, Guesclin and Canterbury rode into the market square of Dinan. As ever, Guesclin had little fear of physical combat. It was a carelessness others dreaded. Canterbury had second thoughts about the duel and offered to return Guesclin's brother without a ransom. 'If he will not fight,' replied the Breton, 'let him surrender to my mercy and present his sword to me, holding it by the point.' This Canterbury would not do. The two knights urged their horses forward and smashed at each other. Sparks cracked beneath their blows. Neither could be cut beneath the armour. Like the Breton wrestlers of his childhood, Guesclin sheathed his sword and grabbed the English knight around the chest, trying to wrench him off his horse. Canterbury's sword fell to the ground. Guesclin dismounted, picked up the sword and threw it into the crowd. He then threw his own after it. The crowd screamed and applauded. Canterbury was still mounted and charged at the Breton, hoping to trample him beneath his animal's hooves. The English horse reared, Guesclin lunged at its belly with his dagger. The horse crashed to the ground with Canterbury beneath it.

Guesclin rushed over to the knight, ripped open his visor and battered the stunned Englishman with his armoured fists.

Seeing the combat was over, English knights jumped into the arena and begged Guesclin to spare Canterbury his life. Intoxicated with adrenalin, Guesclin reluctantly agreed. Lancaster admitted that Guesclin had fought with honour. 'Your brother shall be restored to you,' he declared, 'and I will bestow upon him 1,000 florins. The arms, armour, and horse of the dishonourable knight now belong to you. He shall never be present at my court.' Throughout this account, Jean Cuvelier, the chronicler, repeatedly points out that Guesclin was poorly equipped. Later, when an English herald wishes to see the Breton, Guesclin is mistaken for a brigand rather than a knight, being clad in a plain black tunic with an axe suspended around his neck. Through legendary encounters such as the duel at Dinan and his conduct at the siege of Rennes, the fame of Guesclin grew ever greater. His status as a man of honour was not incompatible with his military role as a guerrilla leader.

Through further deception and craft, Guesclin renewed his attacks on Lancaster's camp. On one occasion, while Lancaster pursued false reports of a relief army, Guesclin invaded his camp, stole all his provisions, and entered Rennes. Lancaster retaliated by erecting a siege tower to bring his costly campaign against Rennes to an end. Sappers began to fill the city moat to allow the tower to be rolled forward against the walls. Before this could be completed, Guesclin led 500 crossbowmen against the tower, setting fire to the great wooden engine. The siege seemed endless. Eventually, Lancaster received news that a truce had been signed between the Kings of England and France. Lancaster was ordered to leave the siege. But the English knight had sworn to take Rennes and he would not break a vow. Word of this reached Guesclin. He understood. It was agreed that Lancaster be allowed within Rennes with 10 knights and place his banner on the battlements. The ludicrous concession was enacted, but as soon as Lancaster had crossed the drawbridge, a triumphant townsman tore down the flag and threw it at his heels.

Rennes made Guesclin's reputation. Charles of Blois personally congratulated Guesclin on his defence of the city. He gave him lordship over La Roche-Derrien and made him a knight banneret. This meant he could replace the swallow-tailed pennon of a knight bachelor for a square flag. Guesclin's name was spoken in the right circles. It came to the attention of the Dauphin Charles. In 1357, the Dauphin granted 'an annual income and pension of 200 pounds of Tours from the revenue of the castle and town of Saint-James-de-Beuvron, to Sir Bertrand du Guesclin, for his loyalty and courage in the defence of Rennes during a long siege.' The Dauphin had assumed French rule in the absence of his father, the French King, captured by the English. As Duke of Normandy also, he was currently battling against Charles the Bad, King of Navarre, owner of vast estates in Normandy, and claimant to the French crown.

To combat Navarre, the Dauphin made Guesclin captain of Pontorson, a frontier town between Normandy and Brittany. The Breton, along with 60 men-at-arms and 60 archers, was to be paid out of royal French coffers. Bouciquaut, the Duke of Normandy's marshal, rode with Guesclin. Together, through cunning, they captured Mantes and Melun, key castles on the Seine. At Melun, Guesclin could not solely rely on craft. While the Dauphin watched at a safe distance, Guesclin despaired of his warriors' tardiness and himself placed a ladder against the castle wall. Bellowing his famous war cry, 'Notre Dame Guesclin', he clambered up the ladder beneath a hail of arrows and stones. Some way up the ladder, a barrel of rocks was tipped over the battlements. The ladder snapped and Guesclin plummeted into the castle moat. He was carried away unconscious, but his bravery made a lasting impression on the Dauphin.

In 1360, the treaty of Bretigny was signed between the Dauphin and the Prince of Wales. The King of England received the vast territory of Aquitaine and Gascony in south-west France, as well as Calais and Ponthieu, a district around the mouth of the Somme. The King of France was released on ransom of three million gold crowns. Later, because one of the agreed hostages broke parole, the King returned to the court of England, thankful to leave the problems of France to his son. It was very much a one-sided treaty, but with the aggression of the King of Navarre, the Dauphin needed the break. Truce, however, did not mean security from English forces. They were left unemployed in France. Consisting of English, Gascon, Navarrese, German, Spanish, and Flemish mercenaries, these companies now acted as independent armies. Terrorising, pillaging, kidnapping, and murdering their way across Normandy, Champagne, Burgundy, and Languedoc, they were posing a greater problem than if they had been under the control of the English King. In Normandy, Guesclin was employed to hunt the rogue companies and did so with much success. In 1362, Guesclin was made *capitaine souverain*, supreme commander of the Duchy of Normandy.

Early in 1364, news arrived of the death of the King of France in England. The Dauphin was crowned Charles V. He made Guesclin *chambellan du roi*. On the eve of Charles' coronation, the King of Navarre concentrated his troops at Evreux in Normandy. They were recruited from the free companies and commanded by Jean de Grailly, captain of the town of Buch. Froissart described his soldiers as 'archers and brigands'. They numbered 700 lances, 300 archers, and 500 other soldiers. Among them were several knights, a banneret from Navarre, and an English knight, Sir John Jouel, who led the largest personal contingent of men-at-arms and archers within the army. Before this main army, Grailly sent out a knight to gather information and conduct frontier war against the French. The reports he received did not please him. A force of 1,500 soldiers was spotted, the majority of them being Bretons led by Bertrand du Guesclin. Alongside him rode knights from Auxerre, Beaumont, Chalon, Beaujeu, the Master of the Crossbows, Baudouin of Annequin, and many warriors from Gascony. 'By

English bowmen at the battle of Crecy, 1346. Such simple wooden bows were not exclusive to the English but common among the French as well. They were inferior in both power and range to the crossbow. From the Chronicles of Froissart in the Bibliotheque Nationale, Paris.

the head of Saint Anthony,' swore Grailly, 'Gascon against Gascon.' He had many Gascon mercenaries in his army and did not relish testing their loyalty.

A few days later, the Navarrese crossed the river Eure and made camp on the hill of Cocherel. After resting, they drew up in their order of battle. Sir John Jouel formed the first battle, surrounded by his English men-at-arms and archers. The second battle was led by Grailly and numbered 400 fighting men including the knight of Navarre. The third battle consisted of 400 warriors led by three French knights. Grailly's banner was placed upon a bush of thorns and guarded by 60 men. The Navarrese waited for the French to attack them. They arrived late on the battlefield. Realising they had already lost the advantage of territory, the French nevertheless prepared for battle in a swampy field with the river behind them. Guesclin and his Bretons formed the first battle. The second was led by the Count of Auxerre and included warriors from Normandy and Picardy. The third battle of Burgundians was led by the Archpriest Arnaud of Cervole. A rearguard was formed by the Gascons. They wished to be allowed to

The taking of Valonges. Guesclin watches one of his warriors carry his standard up to the battlements. Note the so-called longbows used by the French men-at-arms. One of a series of illustrations from a life of Guesclin made about 1400, in the library of Henry Yates Thompson.

concentrate on the taking of Grailly's standard, suggesting a snatch-group of 30 horsemen be organised to capture the enemy commander and bring a quick end to the battle. It was agreed. The French knights then debated who should be commander for the day and what battle-cry they should adopt. The Count of Auxerre was the most senior in rank but he declined, saying there were others more experienced than him. Finally, they agreed that Guesclin was the most competent and he should be obeyed throughout the day's combat.

Having established authority, the French faced the problem of the Navarrese firmly positioned on a hill. It was a very hot day; they were short on provisions. As the French discussed what to do, some prisoners were freed from the Navarrese army. They told the French that Grailly would soon be reinforced and should attack at once. But the French were reluctant to assault such a strong position. The next day, Guesclin suggested an acceptable strategy. 'Let us make preparations to withdraw. Our people are troubled by the heat. The servants and spare horses should be sent back to our camp. If the enemy are impatient to fight then they will come down the hill and we can turn and fight them on more equal terms.' The French knights drew up their standards and the baggage train proceeded to retreat over the river Eure. Guesclin had judged the mood of the Navarrese correctly. Sir John Jouel was tired of waiting. When he saw the French withdrawal, he feared he would be denied a battle altogether. His soldiers had to be paid and he would not let their prize disappear. Grailly was not so impetuous. He suspected a trick. But Jouel could not stand the sight and shouted to his men: 'By Saint George, whosoever loves me, let them join me in my fight with the enemy!' Jouel and his Englishmen dashed down the hill. Grailly would not see his army defeated piecemeal and ordered a general advance.

The French were triumphant. They turned and cried 'Notre Dame Guesclin!' Seeing the ordered French lines, the Navarrese recoiled. Their archers ran to the front. At close range, the arrows were deadly, but the French were largely on foot and protected by warriors carrying large shields. The battle broke into crowds of knights and footsoldiers in fierce hand-to-hand combat. Shortened lances, axes, and swords hacked and tore. When possible, knights were isolated and captured for ransom. But the fighting was bitter and many prominent knights were slaughtered, among them the Master of the Crossbows and the banneret of Navarre. The Archpriest Arnaud had withdrawn to the bridge over the Eure at the beginning of the battle on the pretence of some tactical manoeuvre. In truth he was waiting to see who would triumph. In the meanwhile, Sir John Jouel charged straight at the Bretons and Guesclin. He fought remarkably, was wounded several times, fainted under his wounds, and was taken prisoner, later to die. The Gascons remained committed to their assault on Grailly. The 30 horsemen lunged forward. Grailly defended himself with a great axe. The horsemen pushed into the crowd and finally plucked him from among his men. The Gascons then surged on to his standard. The banner was ripped to pieces. The battle was over. Several knights were captured, but the majority of ordinary Navarrese were slaughtered. It was good news for Charles V on the eve of his coronation. And all thanks to Guesclin. The Breton was made Count of Longueville in northern Normandy, a former property of the King of Navarre.

Guesclin was now 44 and it might be thought he had done enough to deserve retirement, but the warlord's tasks were never over. Constantly in the field against ravaging bands of soldiers in Normandy, there was still the problem of the succession of Brittany to be settled. Since 1343, John, the Montfort heir, had been kept at Edward III's court. In 1362, he was released under heavy obligation to seek his fortune in Brittany. He endeavoured to strike a peace with Charles of Blois, but his wife refused. In the late summer of 1364, the town of Auray, loyal to the Blois cause, was besieged by Montfort. Blois asked Guesclin for help. The Breton, ever faithful to his first master, immediately left Normandy with his victorious army of Cocherel. Blois assembled 2,500 lances. Guesclin was the chief military adviser. Outside Auray, they formed three battles with a rearguard. As usual, Guesclin and his Breton followers formed the first battle, the Count of Auxerre led the second and Blois the third. Each battle consisted of 1,000 fighting men. Montfort's army numbered many Englishmen. The active commander was Sir John Chandos. He organised three battles, each containing 500 men-at-arms and 400 archers. A rearguard of 500 men was placed on the wing to reinforce any group that faltered. Hewe Caurell, the knight placed in charge of this wing, felt ashamed to command reinforcements, preferring to be among the first to fight. Chandos reassured him it was not because he was a bad knight, but because he was wise and was needed to lead such a crucial group. Otherwise Chandos would have to do it himself. The knight accepted the task.

On a plain before Auray, the two armies waited. Last-minute Breton negotiations tried for peace, but Chandos' English soldiers told him they had spent all their money and needed a battle to replenish their resources. Chandos promised not to accept a truce. The two forces closed for battle. The French were dismounted in close order, their shortened lances and spears held by a phalanx of foot soldiers. The English struck the first blow. Their shot did little damage to Frenchmen well protected by shields and armour. The archers cast away their bows and broke into Guesclin's battle, fighting with axes. Blois clashed with Montfort. The English suffered badly but were reinforced by the wing of Hewe Caurell. This proved a turning point. Sir John Chandos hammered the Count of Auxerre. Auxerre's battle crumbled, many fled, he was wounded and captured. Seeing Montfort's warriors in good order, many Frenchmen mounted their horses and left the carnage. But still the Bretons around Guesclin kept fighting. Chandos concentrated on them. Axes swung and bascinets were ripped open. Guesclin was overwhelmed and taken prisoner. The entire French army broke. A valiant few fought a last stand around Charles of Blois. The Blois standard was torn down and the Breton leader slain. The English had agreed beforehand not to spare him for ransom: the civil war had to end. Similarly, the French had agreed not to spare Montfort. The Breton succession had to be settled. On that day it was. Charles V concluded a peace in Brittany and acknowledged Montfort as Duke. In default of male heirs, however, the duchy was to revert to the children of Charles of Blois, thus revealing the French King's true sympathies.

The mercenary companies were again unemployed. They plagued the land, ravaged its resources, threatening to set up independent realms. As many of them were English or foreign with anti-French interests, the problem very much belonged to Charles V. Pope Urban V suggested the best way to rid the land of these parasites was to send them on a crusade. The King of Hungary was keen for help against the Turks. But such a trek involved travel through Germany and the Emperor would not tolerate their presence on his territory. Just then, a crisis developed in Spain. The ruler of Castile was Don Peter, called the Cruel. In his court, his wife had died in mysterious circumstances. She was Charles' sister-in-law. The personal insult was compounded by the political situation. Don Peter was in conflict with the King of Aragon, but Peter had a rival to his crown, Don Henry, who could rely on the support of Aragon and now invited Charles V to his assistance. Finally, the Pope recognised the presence of Jews and Muslims among the supporters of Don Peter and declared the enterprise a crusade. White crosses were sewn over the hauberks of the myriad freebooters in France. They became the White Company. Such a vicious gang of marauders needed a strong leader and Charles could see no one more competent for this post than Bertrand du Guesclin. The Breton was ransomed for 40,000 florins from Sir John Chandos. It is a token of the comfortable respect shown by these two warlords for each other, that Guesclin immediately invited Chandos to join him on the profitable endeavour. Realising the long-term political consequences of this campaign, Chandos declined.

The kind of freelance warrior that rode in Guesclin's army has been recorded by Froissart. One evening, in front of a roaring fire at the court of the Count of Foix, the chronicler listened to the reminiscences of the Bascot de Mauleon. He was not a knight, called a squire by Froissart, but he had arrived like a baron with many followers and several pack animals. His men ate off silver plates. Mauleon was a Gascon of about 55. At the time of Guesclin's expedition to Spain in 1365, he would have been 32. He remembered his career before this. He fought his first battle in his early 20s at Poitiers. He had the good fortune to take prisoner a knight and two squires. This set him up materially, bringing in 3,000 francs of ransom. He next fought in Prussia under Jean de Grailly in the usual sport of warlords, known as the crusade against the Baltic pagans. On their return to France, they rescued noblewomen from the rebellious peasants of the Jacquerie, slaughtering some 6,000: 'They never rebelled again.' From there, Mauleon joined Grailly in the Navarrese war. They pursued a campaign of plunder. 'We became masters of the farmlands and the rivers. We and our friends won a great deal of wealth. But then a truce was made and Mauleon had to leave his captured castles.

'Some of our leaders held a conference about where we should go. We had to live somewhere. We went to Burgundy and had captains of all nationalities: English, Gascon, Spanish, Navarrese, German, Scots. I was there as a captain. There were more than 12,000 of us there along the Loire and in Burgundy. Of that assembly, between 3,000 and 4,000 were really fine soldiers, as trained and skilled in war as any could be. Wonderful men at planning a battle and seizing the advantage. At scaling and assaulting towns and castles. And didn't we show it at the battle of Brignais when we smashed the Constable of France with a good 2,000 lances of knights and squires. This battle was much needed. Before, our men had been poor, now they were rich through prisoners and the towns they took in the archbishopric of Lyons and along the river Rhone.' The mercenary companies caused such aggravation in that area that war broke out between them and the Papacy in Avignon. The Pope invited a Lombard warlord to deal with them. He simply hired the majority of the companies, including the captain Sir John Hawkwood, and took them to Lombardy for his war against the Lord of Milan. A few stayed in France. Mauleon was among them. They made a good living out of ransacking town after town. Then came the campaign of Cocherel and Mauleon rejoined Grailly with a force of 12 lances, attaching himself to the company of John Jouel. Mauleon was taken prisoner but released on ransom, being captured by a cousin. His gang of marauders then suffered badly when ambushed on a raid by the count of Sancerre.

After these set-backs, Mauleon was thankful to join Guesclin's expedition to Spain. He had been present at Auray under the command of Sir Hugh Calverly and now served under him with 10 lances. This was the same Calverly who had been a bitter enemy of Guesclin, but such was the material common interest of knights in the 14th century that both Calverly and Mauleon were happy to accept Guesclin as their leader. Jean de Bourbon, a cousin to Don Peter's dead wife, was figurehead of the French expedition, giving it some legitimacy, but Guesclin was the supreme military commander. The army numbered some 30,000. It marched on Avignon. The Pope gave the expedition his blessing, excommunicated Don Peter, and was compelled to give large sums of money to the ravenous horde. As they disappeared over the Pyrenees, Frenchmen breathed a sigh of relief. The campaign in Castile was fierce and quick. Within a couple of months, several towns had been captured, many Jews slaughtered, and Don Henry crowned king. Don Peter had expediently retreated to Seville. He went in search of powerful allies. In Aquitaine, he secured the support of the Black Prince and through him the King of England. The King of Navarre

The siege of Melun. On the left, Guesclin parleys with the garrison, while on the right, his sappers are undermining the wall. Guesclin's career consisted of many such actions.

lent tacit support by opening the passes of the Pyrenees to the troops of the Black Prince riding with Don Peter to claim back his crown.

At the end of their campaign, the army of Guesclin disintegrated into a rabble of marauders. The Spaniards wanted them no more than the French. Many of the free companies pillaged their way back to France under constant attack from the local Spanish. Guesclin had been rewarded with vast estates in Spain and was in no hurry to leave. In his advance southwards, the Black Prince was accompanied by John Chandos and the King of Majorca who had business to settle with Aragon. Many of the soldiers previously in Guesclin's army were re-hired to fight against him. Guesclin and King Henry advanced into Aragon to meet the invaders.

The Black Prince camped on the border of Navarre and Aragon. Before him rode Sir Thomas Felton, gathering intelligence. He crossed the river Ebro and lodged in the town of Najera. A skirmish between Felton and King Henry's troops encouraged Henry to advance on the Black Prince. The Prince rose to the challenge and had his trumpets call for battle order. He created 300 new knights. Anticipation gave way to evasion. Once Henry

knew the full strength of the Prince's army he decided to wait for Guesclin, who arrived with 3,000 French and Aragonese troops. Skirmishing between scouting parties grew more ferocious. In one encounter Felton and his followers were slain. Food shortages and bad weather wore the Prince down. He moved his army across the Ebro and lodged at Logrono. Henry moved his troops back into the town of Najera. His army had grown considerably, numbering 3,000 barded horses, 7,000 genitors (lightly armed horsemen), 10,000 crossbowmen, several thousand footsoldiers armed with javelins, spears and lances, and 20,000 men-at-arms from Castile, Galicia, Portugal, Cordova, and Seville. Guesclin urged battle. Again, there was more manoeuvring, but finally, outside Najera, Henry prepared his men.

At midnight, on the eve of 3 April 1367, King Henry's soldiers were ordered into the battles they would fight in the next day. The first battle consisted of all the freebooters from France, Provence, and Aragon. They were led by Guesclin and a host of foreign knights and amounted to some 4,000 men-at-arms, well armed and dressed in the French manner. The second battle was led by Henry's brother, Don Tello, and included the genitors, some of them Muslim, and 15,000 horsemen and footsoldiers. They were placed to the left behind the first battle. The third battle was King

The clash of arms at the battle of Auray, 1364. The two leading knights both wear the arms of Brittany, representing their struggle for succession. Guesclin fought alongside Charles of Blois.

Henry's with 7,000 horsemen and several thousand footsoldiers armed with crossbows. In these formations, the men spent the night.

The next day at dawn, banners were unrolled and the Black Prince advanced across hilly scrubland to Najera. John Chandos requested permission to unfurl his own banner: silver field, a sharp pile gules. It was granted and flew alongside the cross of St George. As was the practice of the day, the English and Gascon men-at-arms dismounted. The Black Prince made a short prayer and then proclaimed: 'Advance banners in the name of God and Saint George.' The first battle was led by Chandos and the Duke of Lancaster and clashed with Guesclin's company. Spears and shields broke upon each other. The Black Prince and Don Peter led the second battle against the Spanish. The Spanish company under Don Tello broke immediately. The Black Prince crashed onto the battle of King Henry. Many Spanish were armed with slings and their stones caused serious injuries. The English archers retaliated. On the wings of Henry's battle, the Spanish light horsemen kept good order, dashing in among any gaps, hurling their javelins. As the fighting wore on, many of the ordinary Spanish gave way. The longest held combat was between Guesclin and Chandos. The old rivalry struggled on. Chandos pushed so far into the fray that he was surrounded. Suddenly, a Spaniard leapt upon him. Underneath the big man, Chandos twisted to reach the dagger strapped to his chest. He plunged it into the side and back of the Spaniard until he was free. The English pressed on. With the rout of Don Tello's second battle, King Henry three times rallied his warriors. Eventually, the tide of battle had been determined, King Henry withdrew with his warriors to Najera. Several English and Gascons took to their horses to pursue the Spaniards, breaking into the town and pillaging King Henry's treasure. Guesclin remained on the field and was made a prisoner by Chandos.

The Black Prince was celebrated as the greatest knight in Christendom. Najera joined Crecy and Poitiers as a trinity of historic English victories. But his men were hungry and without pay. Don Peter refused to reward them, insisting that the rabble leave Spain straight away. Most of the French and Spanish prisoners were ransomed for immediate cash, but while the Prince remained in Spain, Guesclin was considered too dangerous to free. The deposed Don Henry gathered support in Aragon and southern France. He raided the territory of the Black Prince. In 1368, with the Prince back in Aquitaine, Guesclin's ransom was set at the huge sum of 100,000 francs. Amazingly, within the month, the sum was paid by the King of France and the Duke of Anjou. Such was the value of this warlord. Guesclin's captivity had been far from harsh. He enjoyed the company of Chandos. He called him 'the most renowned knight of the world'. He recognised him as the true victor of Najera.

The Spanish campaign had cost the Black Prince dearly. He returned to Aquitaine in need of money. He proceeded to raise a tax. Several lords, especially those of Gascony, rejected the tax and gathered at the court of the

King of France. In Aragon, Don Henry thought it timely to reattempt an assault on Castile. He captured the town of Leon and then laid siege to Toledo. Guesclin heard news of the resurgence and took leave from Anjou to join Henry. Popular Spanish support lay with Henry and Don Peter had to request the kings of Portugal and Granada for help. 20,000 Saracen horsemen rode to his banner at Seville and from there Don Peter made for Toledo to raise the siege. Guesclin advised Henry to surprise Peter. Henry took his best men and descended on the castle of Montiel in southern Castile where Peter had spent the night. Peter's forces outnumbered Henry, but the surprise gained him an advantage. With cries of 'Castile for King Henry' and 'Notre Dame Guesclin', Henry crushed Peter's vanguard. Because of the

Edward, the Black Prince, a leading adversary of Guesclin. Detail of the latten effigy in Canterbury Cathedral of around 1376.

great number of Muslims among the enemy, Guesclin had given orders that no prisoners were to be taken. Don Peter rallied and ordered the rest of his men forward. A great battle developed. The Saracens proved particularly fierce, shooting bows and hurling javelins. But Don Peter's army began to break and he was urged to withdraw to the castle of Montiel.

Having obtained the victory, Don Henry laid siege to Montiel. The castle was tough but the surprise of the assault meant it was poorly provisioned. One night, Don Peter crept out of the fortress. The Begue of Villains was on guard and claimed the fugitives as his prisoners. Peter agreed and was taken to his quarters. The news brought Don Henry to the Begue's lodgings. 'Where is that son of a whore and Jew that calls himself the King of Castile?' he bellowed. Out of the gloom, Peter replied: 'No, you are the whoreson and I am the son of King Alphonso of Castile.' He grabbed Henry by the arms and threw him over a bench. He drew a dagger and was about to slay him, when the viscount Rocaberti caught Peter by the leg and tripped him. Henry drew his long knife and plunged it into his brother. Two English knights tried to defend Peter but were cut down. The Don lay dead. The war of the Castilian succession had ended. Guesclin was made constable of Castile and given further estates in Molina and Soria, worth 20,000 francs a year. Henry even tried to entice Guesclin on further adventures by proclaiming him King of Granada. But he was destined not to carry this crusade against the infidels, or even enjoy a warlord's retirement in Spain, In 1370, Charles V recalled Guesclin to France.

Charles V had used the troubled peace since the treaty of Bretigny to strengthen his forces for the war he knew would come. The French crown could not tolerate vast stretches of French land in foreign hands. With the burden of King John's ransom removed, taxes were diverted towards the equipping of a royal army. A powerful artillery train was built up. Paris was surrounded by new walls; a royal navy created. Statutes were passed: they encouraged the practice of archery and crossbow shooting; the organisation of an army into companies under captains led by lieutenants or the constable; and a regular inspection and repairing of important castles. Aside from military organisation, Charles was adept at diplomacy. A marriage ensured friendly relations with Flanders, for so long allied to England, while Charles' support of Don Henry maintained an important Spanish ally. By 1369, over 800 towns and districts in Aquitaine had declared an allegiance to the French crown. In the north, Ponthieu rejected English dominance. The time for war had arrived.

With the retirement of Moreau de Fiennes, Charles V needed a new Constable, a supreme commander of French forces. The victorious activities of Guesclin made him the most obvious candidate. But there was the problem of Guesclin's lowly social status. He himself admitted this when summoned to Paris. 'My lord and noble King,' he explained. 'I am of too low blood to accept the great office of Constable of France. Whoever accepts it must command the most noble men as well as the ordinary. How could I be

so bold to order these lords here, your cousins and relations? Envy should be so great that I would fear it. Is there not some other office I could fulfil?' The King would not accept this. 'Sir Bertrand,' he replied, 'there is neither a brother nor cousin, nor count nor baron in my realm who shall disobey you. And if they do, they shall receive my greatest anger. Take the position I offer you. We need you.' Guesclin was invested with the office of Constable. In order to strengthen his authority, the King placed him next to him at his dinner table and showed him great friendship. In addition, Guesclin and his heirs were given many estates. According to Froissart, the Duke of Anjou was influential in securing Guesclin this position.

In his 50s, Guesclin's energy was no less than it had been in his youth. He conquered the area of Poitou in English-held Aquitaine and captured the town of Poitiers. The port of Rochelle opened its gates to him. In Brittany, Duke Montfort declared for England, but the timing was wrong. The majority of Breton lords favoured the French King. Montfort was forced to flee to England and Guesclin occupied the most important Breton towns. Guesclin's success was partly facilitated by the death of his arch rival Sir John Chandos in 1369 in a skirmish. The weight of victory, however, lay in Guesclin's experience of commanding men and handling the logistical and

The battle of Najera, 1367. According to this illustration, Muslim warriors fought on both sides. The English and French men-at-arms dismounted for the battle.

96

Muslim horsemen confront
14th century knights. In
Guesclin's Spanish
campaigns, Muslim light
horsemen called genitors
were particularly feared.
From the *Histoire du
Voyage et Conquete de
Jerusalem*, 1337, now in
the Bibliotheque Nationale,
Paris.

strategical problems of campaigning. In 1373, Edward III sent an army to Calais. It was confronted by the characteristic guerrilla tactics of Guesclin. According to Froissart, this strategic evasion may have owed much to Chàrles V, despite Guesclin's experience in such warfare. The King of France specifically forbade his men to engage the English in battle. Instead, he set 600 lances to follow and harass the English army. Sometimes, it was claimed, the two forces rode so close that English knights spoke to French knights riding at their flank. 'It's a fine day for hawking,' said one frustrated English knight happening upon a Frenchman. 'Why don't you fly for a kill since you've got wings?' 'That's true,' replied the French knight. 'If it depended on me, we would fly out after you.' But the King of France would not be drawn into a major battle.

Charles' advisers backed him totally: 'Let the English ride on. They cannot rob you of your inheritance. They will grow tired and crumble away to nothing. Sometimes a storm cloud appears over the country, but later it passes on and disperses. So will it be with the English soldiers.' This strategy was clarified and confirmed at a conference in Paris. 'I do not say that the English should not be fought,' advised Guesclin,' but I want it to be executed from a position of advantage. That is what the English did at

Poitiers and Crecy.' Oliver de Clisson, a lieutenant to Guesclin, had spent much time with the English and agreed with his commander: 'The English have won so many major victories that they have come to believe they cannot lose. In battle, they are the most confident nation in the world. In my humble opinion, it would be inadvisable to fight them unless they can be taken at a disadvantage.' The King of France then asked his brother, the Duke of Anjou, for his thoughts. 'Anyone who gives you different advice to what has been said betrays our interests. When the English expect to find us in one part of the country, we shall be in another, and we shall take from them when it best suits us the few pieces of territory they still hold.' Charles V was pleased with this advice. 'Indeed, I have no intention of marching out and hazarding my knights and my kingdom in one encounter for a piece of farmland. I entrust the whole responsibility of my realm to my Constable and his associates.' The intelligence and concordance of French military leadership ensured a victorious campaign.

The Dukes of Lancaster and Brittany plundered their way across France. Several times they sent their heralds to demand battle from the French. Guesclin refused. Frequently the English were forced to camp in open country, while the French tailing them lodged comfortably in friendly castles. The land they passed through had been devastated by marauding companies before them. The English suffered from a lack of food, but they dared not go out foraging. The French had grown to 3,000 lances and would annihilate any raiding parties. The English baggage train, when not ambushed, was ravaged by illness and bad weather. By the time the English army reached Aquitaine, it was useless. Like many of his knights, the English commander contracted a sickness and passed away. At the end of this dismal campaign, Guesclin counter-attacked and captured yet more English territory.

In 1375, a truce was agreed at Bruges. In 1376, the Black Prince died. A year later, he was followed by his father, Edward III. With the principal antagonists out of the way, Charles V surged on with his counter-attack, even taking the fighting against the English coast. Charles the Bad of Navarre remained a source of anti-French conspiracy and the French King moved against him. Guesclin was sent to Normandy to occupy his remaining estates, while King Henry of Castile seized his land in Spain. From there, Charles turned his attention to Brittany. He deposed the Duke of Brittany and annexed the entire country to his royal domain. Such a move was politically insensitive. The Bretons had always considered themselves an independent people and many of Charles', most loyal retainers were Breton, not least of them being Guesclin.

Although Guesclin had sworn to obey the French King, his ultimate loyalty lay with a Brittany independent of both English and French control. But he had vowed to serve the King and he could see the political sense of making Brittany French rather than letting it fall into the hands of the English. As ordered, he rode to Rennes at the heart of his homeland. There

was no fighting. He repeatedly asked the Duke of Anjou to arrange a truce with Brittany. He wanted negotiation. He would not fight his own people. But in the minds of many Bretons, Guesclin had already become a traitor. He had entered Brittany with an army of conquest. He served the King before Brittany. In Paris, the royal court noted the reluctance of Guesclin. They suggested to Charles that Guesclin could no longer be trusted. In order to prove otherwise, and maybe because the King realised Guesclin's dilemma, the Breton was sent to Auvergne in south-east France to quell some marauding soldiers.

At nearly 60, this was a dismal finale to the splendid career of Bertrand du Guesclin. The suspicion of his royal master and the conflict with his homeland must have profoundly saddened Guesclin, loosening his interest in life. In Auvergne, he faced the brigand armies he had fought so many times before. Would they never cease? At last, campaigning tired him. Before the town of Chateauneuf de Randon, Guesclin fell ill. On 13 July 1380, he died. The same day, the castle surrendered. Its keys were placed at the dead warlord's feet. Guesclin's body was taken back to Paris and buried at Saint Denis in a tomb near to that prepared for Charles V. Despite their final disagreement over Brittany, Charles realised his kingdom owed a great debt to Guesclin. The King believed it not wise to broadcast the death of such a powerful man, but at the quiet funeral service words were spoken 'as though he had been the King's son'. A few months later, Charles himself was dead.

The legend of Guesclin grew stronger as the Hundred Years War slowly turned against the French once more. During the reign of Charles VI, nine years after Guesclin's death, a spectacular memorial service was held in his honour. It is believed to have contained the first funeral oration for a layman other than a king or prince. The text took the biblical theme *Nominatus est usque ad extrema terrae*: 'His name is known to the ends of the earth.' Four men, armoured and mounted on fine chargers, entered the church representing the dead warlord as he was when alive. Throughout French court art and literature, Guesclin was added to the list of chivalric heroes known as the Nine Worthies. He was ranked alongside Alexander, Caesar, Arthur, and Charlemagne. In the early 15th century, when the French began their final counter-attack against the English, a gold ring belonging to Guesclin is said to have been given to Joan of Arc. In death, the Breton warlord continued to serve the French kingdom as successfully as he had during his life.

JAN ZIZKA

Jan Zizka had little to lose. The small freehold estate his father had left him could not keep him out of debt. The contract he had signed, confirming the debt, promised hard retribution from the lord of the region, Peter of Rosenberg, the greatest of Bohemian magnates. In 1380, at the age of 20, Zizka sold his land in Trocnov, southern Bohemia, and made for the court of King Wenceslas IV at Prague. He was a pugnacious young man. In a boyhood fight he had lost an eye. Zizka is thought to mean 'one-eyed' and was his name alone in his family.

C.1360—1424

By 1392, Zizka's tough character had earned him the position of Royal Hunter amid the forestland of Zahorany, just south of Prague. The job kept him fit and alert, but above all it enabled him to rub shoulders with the King and principal Bohemian aristocrats. In the blood and bluster of the chase, there was a robust informality. During the Royal hunts, which frequently lasted several weeks, Zizka could study his feudal superiors and make valuable contacts. In 1395, the sport came to an end. Relations between Wenceslas and his leading lords deteriorated. Henry of Rosenberg detained the King for several months at his castle in the south. Rosenberg would not tolerate the centralization of power introduced by the King's father. Eventually, Wenceslas was released but two parties now formed. Rosenberg and his associates were joined by the King's younger brother, Sigismund, King of Hungary, and his cousin, Jost, Margrave of Moravia; Wenceslas could count on the support of his youngest brother, Duke of Gorlitz, and other minor magnates who feared the dominance of Rosenberg.

Jan Zizka, blind in one eye from his youth. Stone portrait made by Wendel Roskopf shortly after 1500, now in the National Museum, Prague.

The two factions recruited armed bands and the next few years saw relentless feuding throughout the country. The once stable and prosperous Czech kingdom was torn by mercenary companies causing the kind of havoc experienced by the French during the Hundred Years War.

Zizka demonstrated his loyalty to his King by joining a military company and ravaging the lands of his former overlord, Rosenberg, in southern Bohemia. By 1405, the conflict had cooled and practical survival overcome aristocratic differences. But still the mercenary gangs scoured the land for plunder. Once created, the monster could not easily be dismantled. In 1409, Zizka himself seems to have gone off the rails, Wenceslas signed a letter of amnesty to the townsmen of Budweis, forgiving Zizka all crimes against the Bohemian kingdom. The same year, Wenceslas and his leading warlord, John Sokol of Lamberg, seized upon a means to rid their land of the marauding warrior bands. As in France, the device was to be a foreign campaign. But this time, it was not a crusade, but a war against crusaders – the Teutonic Knights.

Ever since they had left the Holy Land and transferred their base of operations to the Baltic coast, the martial monastic Teutonic Order had advanced east from the Vistula, conquered Prussia and extended its control over Livonia and Estonia. In alliance with the Hanseatic League, the Teutonic Knights dominated Baltic trade and proved militarily awesome. Each year, nobles and mercenary knights from all over Western Europe joined the Teutonic Order on raids against the pagan inhabitants of the eastern Baltic lands. This systematic extermination of these people, dignified and justified by the title of crusade, was almost regarded as a sport; certainly it was a finishing school for young warriors keen on battle experience. The regular influx of western knighthood kept the Teutonic Order aware of the latest military developments and filled its ranks with highly effective young men. Their annual raids continued to devastate Lithuania even after the country had converted to Christianity in 1387. The true brutality of the Teutonic Order could not be made any plainer.

Poland had originally invited the Teutonic knights to the Baltic coast to rid them of troublesome neighbours. But by the beginning of the 15th century, the Order dominated Polish estates and blocked Poland's access to the Baltic sea. In 1385, Jagello, Grand Duke of Lithuania, had been adopted by the Queen of Poland and married her daughter. He became Wladislaw, King of Poland, and the union of Lithuania and Poland proved a powerful counterbalance to the Teutonic Order. It was not long before the two states clashed. In 1409, the still pagan region of Samogitia rose in revolt against the Teutonic Order. Poland and Lithuania supported the revolt, leaving the Teutonic Grand Master no choice but to declare war on Poland. Both sides prepared for a major conflict in 1410.

Naturally, western knighthood rallied to the 'righteous' cause of the northern crusaders. It still considered the Slavs, Christian or not, as 'Saracens'. Poland could only call upon other Slav nations, principally Bohemia. Relations between the two Kings were not good, but Wenceslas could see no political reason not to send his troops, particularly in the light of Sigismund's declaration against Poland. Amnesties were issued to the leading warrior bands of Bohemia and a good many enrolled in Sokol's mercenary army. In Bohemia, there was a deep hatred between the Slavic Czech natives and German immigrants who usually formed the richer, merchant classes. A war in alliance with Polish Slavs against Teutonic Germans encouraged good morale in the warrior bands riding to the standard of the King of Poland. Among these adventurers, Zizka led his own gang of veteran guerrilla fighters.

Wladislaw's army of 1410 consisted of Polish and Lithuanian knights and their retainers, Sokol's Bohemian mercenaries, and the Tatar followers of Witold, governor of Lithuania. The Tatar numbers were not great, but the Germans overemphasised their contribution to the Polish army in order to

Knights of the Teutonic Order battling with Poles and Lithuanians. From Ward Lock's *Illustrated History of the World*, 1885.

104

create the impression of a pagan enemy. The Polish forces gathered at Czerwinsk on the Vistula, not far from Warsaw. To divert the Teutonic knights from their true path of attack, Wladislaw ordered raids into western Prussia and along the north-east frontier of the Teutonic realm. In July 1410, the Polish army crossed the Vistula by means of a pontoon bridge and advanced northwards into central Prussia. In the meantime, Ulrich von Jungingen, Teutonic Grand Master, awaited the arrival of mercenary troops, among them English bowmen and Genoese crossbowmen. Although commanding a smaller force, von Jungingen was well aware of the superior professionalism of his warriors opposed to the massed, but amateur feudal peasant levies that swelled the Polish ranks. 'Witold's men are more at home with a spoon than a sword,' he sneered.

Marienburg was the castle headquarters of the Teutonic Order and the Poles headed straight for it. Von Jungingen blocked their advance at a site near Kurzetnik. He heavily fortified the nearby riverbanks with palisades and awaited Wladislaw. The Polish King knew better than to attack and sought to outflank the Teutonic army. The Grand Master was determined to bring the Poles to battle and crossed the river Drweca. The armies converged on the open ground between the villages of Tannenberg and Grunwald. The site suited both commanders very well as they both placed great faith in their horsemen. The Poles and Lithuanians numbered some 29,000 horse and 10,000 footsoldiers; the Teutonic army included 21,000 horsemen and about 6,000 footsoldiers.

Handgunners from the *Rudimentum Noviciorum*, Lubeck, 1475. By the early 15th century, firearms were a vital aspect of battle and Zizka soon mastered their employment.

The Teutonic Order was early to rise and their ready formations surprised Wladislaw. As the Polish King attended Mass, Witold and the Polish commanders assembled warriors around 50 Polish banners and 40 Lithuanian banners. Within the Polish contingent, two of these banners consisted entirely of Bohemian soldiers, while a further three contained a good many. Their presence, however, was more important than their numbers. Wladislaw was so impressed by the reputation of Sokol that he offered him overall command of the Slavic army. The Bohemian warlord courteously refused. But throughout the battle, Sokol remained at the King's side. Von Jungingen did not want to initiate the battle: he had dug ditches, erected obstacles, and entrenched his cannon. This gave the Poles time. After three hours of skirmishing, the impatient Grand Master sent forward a party of knights. Refusing to address the Polish King by his title, they offered him their swords: 'We give you these weapons so that you may begin the battle and cease to hide in the woods.' The King and his followers were outraged. A general advance was ordered.

The Lithuanians on the right wing of the Polish army could not restrain themselves. They dashed forward on their small ponies, outstripping the more orderly Polish centre. They overran the Teutonic footsoldiers and cannon, but were soundly stopped by the Germanic men-at-arms. In the centre of the battle, the Teutonic cannon boomed, followed by the thunderous trotting of the Knights of the Order. Whooping, yelping Polish and Tatar horsemen raced to meet them. As collision seemed imminent, the horses of both sides began to shy away from impact. Some slowed down, others tried to pull back, but the blind horses behind urged them on. The formations of the initial charge broke up. By the time both sides made contact, the warriors clashed in little groups scattered across the battlefield. Apparently the more lightly armoured Lithuanians and Tatars were unable to use their steppe tactics to their advantage and suffered in hand-to-hand conflict with knights in plate armour. The Polish right wing wavered and broke. Witold begged Wladislaw to show himself to the remaining warriors to arouse their morale. The King rode among his army. But the Grand

Master piled on the pressure on the Polish centre and sent in his reserves.

The presence of both Wladislaw and Witold on the battlefield reached many of the routed Lithuanians. They reorganised and returned to the battle, hitting the Teutonic army in the rear. Suddenly, the greater numbers of the Slavs began to tell and the Germans were surrounded. In the final struggle, the Bohemians are said to have distinguished themselves. There is no record of Zizka at this battle, but a major combat such as this was a rare occurrence a professional soldier could not afford to miss. Zizka was not getting any younger and he may have considered this battle his last chance to win prisoners, booty, and perhaps some professional acclaim. By early evening, however, there was little opportunity for sparing high-ranking prisoners for ransom. The bitterness between Slav and German ensured that few beaten warriors survived. In the chaos of defeat, the Teutonic Grand Master was slain along with other principal Knights of the Order. The fortified Teutonic camp was quickly overcome. Among the booty were wagons loaded with barrels of wine. To prevent the mass intoxication of his army, Wladislaw ordered the barrels broken and amazingly he was obeyed. Also uncovered in the enemy camp were piles of grease-covered torches with which the Germans had hoped to pursue the defeated Poles into the night. They were now snatched up by the Tatars and Lithuanians hunting the fleeing Germans.

The victorious Poles named the battle after the village of Grunwald, whereas the Germans remembered it as Tannenberg. Five hundred years later, the Germans defeated the Russians on the Eastern Front in 1914. That battle took place nowhere near the medieval site, but the Germans seized upon the name of Tannenberg and proclaimed the victory as a national act of revenge against the Slavs. Certainly, the battle of 1410 was a major defeat for the Teutonic Order and heralded their subsequent decline. In the campaigning following the battle, there is a specific reference to Zizka. Wladislaw went on to capture several castles. Zizka is mentioned as one of Sokol's subordinate commanders in charge of defending the newly captured castle of Radzin. A group of Teutonic knights attempted to storm the fortress but Zizka held on to it, winning the notice he seems not to have gained at Grunwald.

Zizka emerged from the Grunwald campaign a wiser and highly experienced soldier. Polish warfare was determined largely by its geography and Zizka learned much about cavalry warfare. But the Poles also adopted western technology. Against European enemies, they placed their crossbows, handguns, and cannon behind fieldworks. In the more mobile warfare of the eastern plains, however, earthworks were useless. Traditionally, transport wagons had been drawn up into a circle – a laager – to protect camps against Tatar horsemen. Inevitably, these wagons were reinforced and used as frontline defences for footsoldiers bearing firearms and bows. The impetus for this development derived from the increased presence of cannon and handguns on the battlefield at the beginning of the

15th century. Giles Fletcher described a Russian version of these mobile fieldworks used against Tatars in his 16th century account *Of the Rus Commonwealth*.

'If there is to be a set battle, or any great invasion by the Tatars, then footsoldiers are set within the running or moving castle, called *vezha* or *guliai-gorod*. This moving castle is so constructed that it may be set up at whatever length is required. It is nothing else but a double wall of wood to defend them on both sides, behind and before, with a space of 3 yards or thereabouts betwixt the two sides, so that they may stand within it and have room enough to charge and discharge their pieces and other weapons. It is closed at both ends and made with loopholes on either side to lay out the nose of their piece or to push forth any other weapon. It is carried with the army wheresoever it goes, being taken into pieces and laid on carts. It is erected without the help of any carpenter or instrument, because the timber is so framed to clasp together one piece within another.'

Hearing of the destructive impact of such devices on large groups of horsemen, Zizka probably considered it interesting but of little use. So long as he was employed by his King, he and his men-at-arms would continue to

Zizka leading his troops. From the beginning of the Hussite movement, Zizka was a popular leader and favourite of the common people. He carries his famous dagger-in-fist mace. Woodcut from an early 15th century edition of Aeneas Sylvius' *Historia Bohemica*.

fight as horse-warriors. Only large armies of footsoldiers, such as rebellious peasants, would require such defences in central Europe. Zizka returned to Bohemia not only rich in experience, but laden with booty. In 1414, he bought a house in the New Town, the Gothic quarter of Prague, not far from the Royal court. He appears to have been employed by the King as an officer of the palace guard, a suitable job for a semi-retired soldier. Frequently, Zizka was responsible for the personal safety of the Royal Family. He regularly accompanied the Queen on her visits to the Chapel of Bethlehem. There they heard the preaching of John Hus.

In a crowded church, Hus spoke out against the corruption of Papal Catholicism. He derided the comfortable life of establishment clergy and demanded a moral decency based simply on the teachings of Christ. It was a common criticism in the 14th and 15th centuries, and a ready congregation pleaser. With three Popes simultaneously occupying the divine throne, how could anyone respect the Catholic hierarchy? But this was not all Hus evoked. Throughout his service hymns were sung. Previously, hymns had been reserved for processions and at the end of sermons. Now, Hus brought singing into the very heart of his service and, above all, the hymns were sung in Czech. This embraced the ordinary, illiterate townsmen as well as the sophisticated courtiers of King Wenceslas. Everyone was raised in a surge of religious reformation combined with Czech national pride. The Czech resentment of German influence in Bohemia has already been stated. Many Bohemians of German background filled positions of power, while the majority of the lower classes were Slavic. In 1409, King Wenceslas ruled that the German element at the University of Prague – the intellectual and religious decision maker – should not be allowed to constantly outvote the Czech faction.

Within Prague, Archbishop Zbynek was chief supporter of Papal authority. Public rows between Zbynek and Hus grew in intensity until the Archbishop excommunicated Hus. The King wished for a quiet life, but public opinion remained excited by his presence. In 1412, he was advised to leave Prague. For the next two years, Hus preached throughout the south of Bohemia, often in the open air. Thus, he widened support for his beliefs among the provincial nobility and rural lower classes. During this activity, Zizka, a Czech of humble background, must have found the teachings of Hus a welcome and overdue expression of all the resentment he had felt towards Germanic overlords. In 1414, an international Catholic conference at Constance in Switzerland demanded that Hus justify his critical beliefs in their presence. King Sigismund of Hungary guaranteed him safe conduct. The meeting became a trial and in 1415 the troublesome Hus was burnt at the stake as a heretic.

Ever after, Sigismund tried to excuse his role in this deception and entrapment. But in the minds of most Bohemians, his broken vow of safe conduct only added to the national outrage of all Czechs. It was probably this aspect, rather than Hus' religious beliefs, that encouraged 452 lords and knights, the majority of Bohemian nobility, to sign an agreement protesting the decision of the Council of Constance and guaranteeing freedom of Hussite preaching on their estates. Defiance of the Council continued when the University of Prague encouraged the giving of both wine and bread in the Eucharist to laymen of both sexes – previously wine had only been allowed to the clergy. A Church of Bohemia had arisen. In the rural communities of the south, followers of Hus took more radical views and founded a group known as the Taborites. Inspired by open air congregations, they took their name from the biblical Mount Tabor. They believed only in what the Bible specifically stated and dispensed with all other religious ritual.

Wenceslas feared for his royal authority and tried to back-track. Hussite churches were closed, but this only encouraged the more committed Hussites to leave Prague for the Taborite communities. Wenceslas was losing control of the situation. As the peasants massed in southern Bohemia, the underprivileged townsmen of Prague were excited by illegal sermons promising them a better life. John Zelivsky, a former monk and acclaimed leader of the street people, realised the inevitability of an armed clash. He needed professional advice and asked a dedicated court follower of the Hussite movement – Jan Zizka. Still chief of security within the royal household, Zizka joined a crowd of Hussite protestors in July 1419. After a powerful sermon by Zelivsky, the angry crowd marched through Prague and broke into the Church of St Stephen where they celebrated Mass in the Hussite manner. They then crowded into the Cattle Market in front of the New Town Hall. The town councillors were asked to release citizens imprisoned in the Hussite crack-down. The councillors refused. A stone was thrown from a window of the Town Hall. The mob exploded. Doors were broken down and councillors thrown out of the building onto the market square where they were slain. The Town Hall was occupied by armed men. Zizka probably commanded the operation.

Throughout this action, Zizka did not believe he was betraying the King. He knew the court favoured Hussite tenets but were compelled by external politics to call a halt to the more radical elements. Zizka had no political commitments. He followed only the truth of God and believed the King would eventually succumb to this righteousness. To the King, however, this was insurrection that threatened his crown. While the Hussites consolidated their position in the New Town, Wenceslas sought help. His court was impatient with the King's mishandling of the crisis and broadly sympathetic to the Hussites. In desperation, Wenceslas called upon his brother, Sigismund of Hungary. The Hussites offered their renewed loyalty to the King in return for recognition of their status. But the shock of the events had been too much for Wenceslas. He suffered a stroke and died. His people were left now to make their own decisions. The lack of royal authority encouraged revolutionary thoughts.

As the only remaining member of the Luxemburg dynasty, Sigismund

At Tabor, Zizka oversaw the conversion of peasant tools into deadly weapons. The most characteristic polearm of the Hussites was the fearsome flail.

was natural heir to the throne of Bohemia. As King of Hungary and Holy Roman Emperor, his energies were concentrated on other problems, especially Turkish incursions into the Balkans. Nevertheless, Sigismund was attracted to the country to which he had so long been an enemy. For the Hussites, and Czechs generally, there could be no worse candidate for the Bohemian throne. Only a few years previously, Sigismund had founded the Order of the Dragon, a crusading elite dedicated to the destruction of heretics and infidels. Zelivsky seized upon the devilish imagery of the Order in his sermons. Sigismund was the Great Red Dragon of the Apocalypse cast down from Heaven by holy brothers who do 'not hold their lives too dear to lay them down'. Here was a pledge in the Bible to do away with the Dragon of Sigismund even at the cost of one's own life. In an atmosphere of radical change, such fantastic imagery seemed the literal truth.

As the majority of Bohemian nobility supported the Hussite cause, a list of demands was presented to Sigismund: freedom of religious practice; freedom from foreign control; Czech should be the official language of Bohemia. Sigismund was preoccupied with campaigns against the Turks and avoided any definite response to the Czechs. Wenceslas' Queen ruled as regent. Sympathetic to the Hussites, she was also concerned with maintaining royal law and order. Garrisons in Prague were filled with German mercenaries and Taborites forbidden entry into the city. News of an ambush on Taborite pilgrims by a Catholic nobleman outside Prague angered the citizens. In a few days of street fighting, Zizka-led Hussites stormed all the royal garrisons and secured the freedom of Prague for their more radical comrades. Zizka now rode west at the invitation of the city of Plzen. Western Bohemia was fervently Hussite and Zizka felt confident of building an army there to oppose the feared arrival of Sigismund. Several nobles joined Zizka and accepted his command despite his lowly status. Kutna Hora, a largely German mining community in eastern Bohemia, became the centre of Catholic opposition. All Hussite inhabitants of the city were massacred. There would be no quarter on either side.

The Catholics put pressure on the Hussites straight away. Skirmishing around Plzen developed into a constricting siege. Within the city, factions among the community suggested to Zizka they could not withstand the conflict. Reluctantly, he signed an armistice with the Catholics and left the city. He now made for Tabor, the newly established town of the Hussite extremists. With these fanatics, Zizka felt more certain he could create an army. As the small force made its way southwards, the Catholics broke their truce and tried to ambush Zizka before he reached Tabor. Fortunately, his scouts gave Zizka good warning. With only 400 men, he sought a strong defensive position. Using the banks of drained fish ponds as earthworks and then drawing his ordinary supply wagons up on the flank and rear, Zizka compelled the 2,000 Catholic men-at-arms to attack his well-prepared frontal position. The horsemen dismounted, but by evening the hand-to-hand fighting had got the Catholics nowhere and they withdrew. The

111

skirmish at Sudomer raised the morale of Zizka's troops and began his reputation as a giant-killer.

At Tabor, Zizka organized the community along military lines. Four captains, *hejtman*, were elected: Zizka, Nicholas of Hus, a senior leader of the Hussite movement, Zybnek of Buchov and Chval Repicky of Machovice, both competent commanders and faithful Taborites. The four men discussed military decisions but Zizka was the senior commander. In the few months Zizka was at Tabor in 1420, he established the new army he wanted. Raids were carried out on nearby Catholic castles that not only gained military experience for the Taborites but also much-needed stocks of equipment, weapons, and horses. The most ingenious developments, however, took place within Tabor. Peasant tools were converted into weapons. Scythes, forks, and hammers became deadly polearms. Of all the agricultural weapons, it was the flail, used to thresh grain, that became the most characteristic of Hussite arms and the most feared by their enemies. Reinforced with iron bands, chains, nails, and studs, flails were carried by special contingents of warriors practised in the sweeping, swiping strokes of the terrible weapon.

In addition to individual arms, Zizka oversaw the conversion of peasant carts into his famous war wagons. Until his followers had more horses, he knew his army would consist largely of foot soldiers and they had to be protected from the eastern European horsemen of Sigismund. The outsides of ordinary wagons were strengthened with wooden boards. Sometimes the boards were in turn reinforced with iron strips and given loopholes through which bowmen and handgunners could shoot. Within the wagons, tools and equipment were carried to clear roads and dig earthworks. One contemporary account mentions each wagon containing 'two axes, two spades, two pickaxes, two hoes, and two shovels.' In battle, chains linked the wagons together with pavises or stakes placed in the gaps. As the Hussite war progressed, the war wagon became the basic organisational unit around which the foot soldiers concentrated. Each wagon was expected to hold two handgunners, six crossbowmen, two flail-carriers, four halberdiers, two shield-carriers, and two well-armed drivers. But such set tactics had still to be formalised and the offensive use of these wagons lay in the future. In 1420, Zizka simply considered them a necessary defence. The presence of handguns in large numbers, which also became characteristic of Hussite warfare, cannot have been expected at this early stage. Bowmen were still the principal source of fire-power.

At the beginning of 1420, King Sigismund had entered Moravia, the south-east region of the Bohemian kingdom. He tried to win over the Bohemian nobility, but they would not forget his insult to their country, his broken vow, and his accusation of heresy. On 1 March, Sigismund did away with negotiation. A Papal bull proclaimed a crusade against the Hussites. Sigismund mobilised a substantial army. German noblemen and mercenaries flocked to his standard. The bull urged all heretics to be killed and their

Hussite wagon fortress. The chalice and goose emblems of the Taborites are illustrated, as are their firearms, crossbows and flails. The wheels of the wagons are chained together to make a stable base. Pen and wash drawing from a Viennese manuscript of the mid 15th century.

possessions confiscated. This was an open licence to murder and pillage at will. What soldier could resist it? A combined knight and peasant army motivated by a religious and nationalist passion might seem a powerful antidote to this pack of German mercenaries. But the Bohemian nobility were nervous of the trained and efficient army of Taborites. Their successful raids on castles and monasteries were unsettling. Cenek of

113

Wartenberg, a devoted Hussite and leading aristocrat, was the first to crack.

In return for minor religious concessions, Wartenberg offered Sigismund Hradcany castle, the defending bastion of Prague. The townsmen of Prague were outraged. They tried to storm the fortress but failed. Sigismund made a triumphant entry into Kutna Hora. Fearing his approach, an armistice was signed between Prague and the Hungarian King. But Sigismund demanded unconditional surrender. Prague was desperate and called upon Zizka. The Taborites responded keenly and advanced swiftly on the capital. Warriors from Hradcany and Sigismund's army tried to intercept Zizka but failed to break his wagon fortress. The reception for Zizka's troops in Prague was ecstatic. The Taborites were less enthusiastic about the townsmen: their puritanism shocked by mercantile wealth. Immediately, Zizka reinforced his tight discipline and compelled warriors to attend daily sermons in which the righteousness of their Holy War was preached.

The most immediate threat to Prague was the garrison in Hradcany, on the western side of the city. Zizka ambushed a supply train sent by Sigismund to the castle. The Hungarian King could not afford to lose the

Zizka plans his campaign within a Hussite wagon fortress.

114

valuable foothold. His army approached Hradcany in battle order. Zizka left his general defence of the city and prepared to confront the King. As the two armies faced each other, Sigismund sent food wagons to the Hradcany garrison and thus forced Zizka to abandon his planned assault. Sigismund tightened his hold around the city and cut the roads into Prague one by one. This, Zizka could not allow. He took his stand on Vitkov hill, a narrow ridge just outside the city commanding two routes eastwards. Vineyards covered the southern slope and an old watchtower stood on the summit. Zizka added earthworks and wooden fortifications. Trees and buildings were knocked down to deprive the enemy of cover.

On 14 July, Sigismund's army was ready. Adventurers from all over Europe swelled the force to 80,000. Bohemians, Germans, Hungarians, and eastern Europeans all assembled under the red crusader cross. Principal among Sigismund's military commanders was the condottiere Philippo Scolari. A Florentine by birth, Scolari, better known as Pippo Spano, had taken keenly to the cavalry warfare of the Hungarians and learned the brutality and craft of frontier fighting against the Turks. When he returned to Italy, contemporaries were shocked by his rigorous, ruthless methods. All his prisoners had their right hands chopped off before being released. It was probably Spano who derived the ingenious relief of Hradcany. Now he brought his murderous skills to bear on Prague. Swiftly, while Zizka and the majority of his men rested in the city, a few thousand Hungarian and Geman horsemen rode up the north-east slope of Vitkov hill. They captured the watchtower and then assaulted the recently built barricades. A small Hussite garrison of 26 men and 3 women bravely defended the wood fort. With no bows or guns, they threw stones and spears at the attackers.

Hearing the alarm, Zizka quickly roused himself and made for the danger with his veteran bodyguard. The rest of the Taborite army followed up the southern slope. Climbing over the tangled remains of vineyards, the Taborite army struck the Germans in the flank. Hussite priests strode forward with religious banners bearing the Chalice of the Host. Behind them were archers, and behind them, warriors wielding flails, pikes, and other polearms. Just as singing had been a vital element in Hussite services, so singing raised the fighting spirit of the Taborites.

'You warriors of God and His Law, pray for God's help and believe in him, so that with him you will ever be victorious. You archers and lancers of knightly rank, pikemen and flailsmen of the common people, keep you all in mind the generous Lord. You baggage boys and advance guards, keep in mind that you do not forfeit your lives through greed and robbery, and never let yourselves be tempted by booty. You all will shout "At them, at them!" and feel the pride of a weapon in your hands, crying "God is our Lord!"'

Before the fanatical Taborites, the Germans and Hungarians broke. Many tumbled down the steep north side. Sigismund's losses were only a few hundred, but were severe enough to deter him from any further assaults.

Zizka's warriors fell to their knees on Vitkov, giving hymns of thanks. The day after the battle, the hill's fortifications were strengthened and ever after it bore the name Zizkov. A long siege of Prague now seemed out of the question. It was either an immediate all-out attack or nothing. Catholic Bohemian nobles did not favour a devastating blow against their capital. In negotiations with Sigismund, they persuaded the King it was not worth the cost. As a sign of their support of the Catholic cause, Sigismund was crowned King of Bohemia on 28 July in the Cathedral of Hradcany. By the end of the month, disease and frustration broke up Sigismund's army. With a final payment of booty ripped out of Hradcany, the mercenary forces were ordered home. The first crusade against the Hussites was over.

With the removal of an outside threat, the split between radical and moderate Hussites led to conflict within Prague. By August, Zizka and his Taborite army left the capital and returned southwards. They carried out a guerrilla war against the castles of Ulrich of Rosenberg. Once created, Zizka's fighting machine could not easily be stopped. Having forced Rosenberg into a truce, Zizka began a campaign against the Plzen region in early 1421. Action took place close to the borders of Bavaria and the Upper Palatinate. The Germans feared uprisings in their own countries. As Holy Roman Emperor, Sigismund had to see to the protection of his Imperial vassals. He ordered a counterattack, but the Taborites allied with the Praguers and the King declined the conflict, withdrawing to Hungary. Zizka renewed his attack on Plzen and established control over western and north-west Bohemia. Atrocities on both sides led to the massacring of thousands of innocent Bohemians.

After a pause in Prague, Zizka turned his attention to eastern Bohemia. Terror encouraged many towns to submit before the Taborites reached them. Even Kutna Hora, the base for Sigismund's operations, surrendered. Finally, Hradcany was besieged and the thorn removed from the side of Prague. As Zizka's success grew, so he changed his name to acknowledge the faith that fired him and his men. He dispensed with Trocnov and called himself Jan Zizka of the Chalice. His former family arms of a crab were replaced by the Chalice of the Taborites.

Battles against recalcitrant townsmen and invading German neighbours kept the Taborites busy throughout the summer of 1421. During one siege, Zizka received a serious wound. Directing operations against the castle of Bor, an arrow through remarkable accident struck Zizka in his right eye, the one not already blind. Surgeons tried to save the eye but infection left Zizka blind and seriously ill. For a man in his 60s, this was a terrible blow to his health. Yet the mere presence of Zizka in his Taborite army discouraged enemy forces and kept his own men confident.

At Kutna Hora in September 1421, a Hussite council of regency offered the crown of Bohemia to Witold of Lithuania. King Wladislaw of Poland had already been offered kingship but declined. Witold remained open to the offer and these negotiations must have profoundly irritated Sigismund.

Pillaging and firing of a Czech village during the Hussite wars. The common people of Bohemia suffered terribly from mercenary German and Hungarian warriors. Drawing from a contemporary 15th century chronicle.

Throughout the autumn of 1421, he gathered a mainly Hungarian army, under the command of Pippo Spano. In October, Pippo crossed the border into Moravia. Sigismund followed and met with German troops from Silesia, Lusatia, the archbishop of Olomouc and Duke Albert of Austria. Several Czech lords, including Ulrich of Rosenberg, rode to Sigismund's banner. Kutna Hora was the inevitable target for the Hungarians. Zizka hurried to its defence. By December, the Taborites were camped outside the city and preparing to confront Sigismund in the open. Zizka commanded the arrangement of his war wagons and 10,000 men took their positions among them. By this stage, the Taborites had acquired many cannon and handguns and were skilled in their use.

Pippo Spano favoured a cavalry assault against the Taborites. His 30,000 soldiers included a majority of Hungarian and Romanian horsemen. He tried to outflank Zizka's right side. Again and again, the Hungarian horsemen rode around the Taborite laager, trying to penetrate any gap or weakness. On each occasion, the Czechs let fly with a blast of handguns and cannon. By nightfall, it seemed as though Zizka could claim another victory. But

117

VS PHILIPPVS HISPANVS DESCOLARIS · RELATOR VICTORIE THEVCRO·

Pippo had not been so silly as to rely on a cavalry attack against a fortified position. In truth, Pippo had only ordered these assaults to keep the Czechs locked within their wagons. His spies revealed to him that the strong German population within Kutna Hora was guarded only by a small Taborite garrison. Under cover of dark, Pippo sent horsemen past Zizka's right flank to the western city gate. Citizens let them in and began a slaughter of the Taborites.

Zizka had not placed his entire army within Kutna Hora as he did not want to chance a long siege. He had hoped to break the Hungarians in one decisive conflict. But now the loss of the city meant that Zizka was isolated and effectively besieged anyway. His fortified camp held few provisions. Zizka had to counter surprise with surprise and go on the offensive. Horses were harnessed to wagons, and before daybreak the Taborite wagon fort broke ground, rumbling towards Sigismund's lines. When the wagons came within range of the Hungarians, the horses halted and the Czechs fired their guns and shot their bows. A breach was smashed through Sigismund's ring. A mile on, the wagons reformed a square and awaited the pursuing Hungarian cavalry. They never came. Sigismund was happy with his possession of Kutna Hora and would not risk any further engagement with Zizka. The Czech warlord had demonstrated the offensive capabilities of the war wagon, tactics that would be developed further throughout the Hussite wars.

As far as Sigismund was concerned, his campaign was over. His men were sent out to winter billets in surrounding villages. For Zizka, winter meant nothing. He simply awaited reinforcements and in early January struck back. The Taborites defeated a group of enemy soldiers in the nearby town of Nebovidy and marched on Kutna Hora. Pippo Spano realised there was little time to concentrate his troops. He advised Sigismund to evacuate the city. Before he went, the King ordered its complete destruction. Fortunately, Zizka's advanced cavalry forces reached Kutna Hora in good time to extinguish the flames. At first, Sigismund's retreat resembled a rout, but after two days he decided on a stand near the village of Habry. Pippo did not think it wise, morale was low among his soldiers. Sigismund remained obstinate and formed battle lines. Again, unusually, the Taborites took the offensive. Their onrush broke the Hungarians. Now the retreat was a rout. Many warriors died crossing frozen rivers that gave way under their weight. Sigismund was thrown out of Bohemia. The failure sickened him and discouraged crusading plans for several years. As for Zizka, the victory meant official recognition as commander-in-chief of all Hussite forces in Bohemia.

With the expulsion of Sigismund, politics again drove a wedge between radical and moderate Hussites. In the spring of 1423, Zizka could no longer tolerate the more extreme views of his Taborite comrades. He rode with his closest followers to eastern Bohemia and assumed command over the Orebite community, establishing a second Tabor. He invited local nobles and knights to join what amounted to a military brotherhood. He composed a military code for his followers in which order and discipline were stressed: soldiers must remain in the battle groups to which they were assigned; van, rear and flanks must be guarded while marching; fires must not be lit without permission; before every undertaking, the army must kneel down and pray to God. Everyone, from lord to peasant, was equal according to God's law and anyone committing a crime on campaign received equal punishment. Booty was to be pooled and divided justly. Anyone keeping booty to himself would be executed. Under this code, Zizka created an army as effective as the original Taborites.

The independence of the Taborites had long irritated Prague. The emergence of Zizka's Orebite community in a similar style compounded the break between the capital and its chief warlord. Hradec Kralove became the centre of the Orebite region and Prague tried to establish some hold over it by placing their own representative as ruler of the town. In the summer of 1423, Zizka expelled the puppet governor. An army of Praguers left their campaigning in Moravia and rushed to confront Zizka. 'Ark against Ark' was how a chronicler described the conflict. In a battle outside Hradec, Zizka broke the Praguers and personally killed their leading priest. Shocked chroniclers recall that the holy man was brought before Zizka and in a fit of rage the warlord smashed his fist-shaped mace on the priest's head. Civil war broke out. The alliance of some Catholic noblemen with Prague intensified the bitterness.

At the beginning of 1424 occurred the sad sight of Zizka's angry army before Prague. He had spent that spring marching through northern and western Bohemia gathering supporters from all major cities. He intended to return to his base at Hradec, but Prague and her allies decided to intercept him while they possessed superior forces. About 15 miles north-east of Prague, Zizka arranged his war wagons on a low hill. He was hemmed in within the bend of a river and the Praguers felt confident. That night, boats and rafts ferried Zizka across the river to freedom. The exasperated Praguers pursued him eastwards. At Malesov, familiar territory near Kutna Hora, Zizka turned to face his hunters. Again he chose a hill for his wagon fort. But this time he ordered his supply wagons to be filled with stones. When only half the Praguers rode into view, they rashly assumed battle formations and advanced up the slope. Zizka commanded his footsoldiers to roll the rock-filled wagons forward, down the hill. The wagons trundled down the slope, gathering speed, finally tipping over and smashing into the Praguers. Their formations broken, Zizka ordered his guns to fire. As the smoke cleared, Orebite horsemen burst out from among the wagons and completed the chaos. The rout destroyed the rest of the Praguers before they even reached the battlefield: 14,000 enemy were slain and all their arms and booty captured. Eastern Bohemia remained under Zizka's control.

In September, Zizka threatened Prague. An armistice prevented conflict. Political agreements followed and Zizka and Prague sealed a fresh alliance

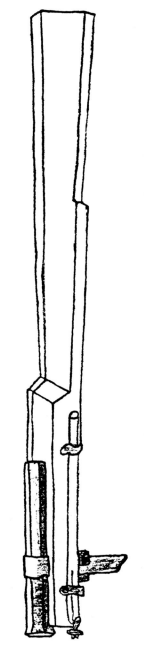

Drawing of a 15th century handgun now in the National Museum, Prague. Length of barrel 30 cm, overall length 113 cm.

Drawing of a 15th century handgun from Plzen in western Czechoslovakia. Length of barrel 30 cm, overall length 105 cm.

Fantastic 16th century version of Zizka's war wagons. His way of war influenced many eastern European and German warlords.

with a new campaign. Moravia remained outside Hussite control even though it formed part of the Bohemian kingdom. A Hussite army of Orebites, Praguers, and Taborites began the march to Moravia in October. On the way, they paused to besiege the castle of a Catholic lord. As preparations were made to assault Pribyslav, Jan Zizka fell ill. He was 64 and had never recovered full fitness since he had lost his sight. He was believed to have contracted plague. Within days, he was dead. Among his last words, he is said to have instructed his lieutenants to 'continue fighting for the love of God and steadfastly and faithfully defend the Truth of God for eternal reward'. Grief racked the entire Hussite army. Zizka's followers proclaimed themselves Orphans, and under this name fought on.

Zizka's body was buried at Hradec Kralove. The subsequent disappearance of his tomb inspired several legends. One story maintains that Zizka asked for his dead body to be flayed and the skin made into a drum that would forever lead his warriors. In reality, Zizka's greatest legacy was his method of war. Until the final defeat of the radical Hussites in 1434, the Taborites and Orphans continued the success of his tactics in battle after battle. On their banners, the warriors painted an image of Zizka in armour on a white horse, holding his famous fist-shaped mace. Wherever the Hussites carried this standard, they were said to be invincible. Even in death, Zizka led his army to victory.

VLAD DRACULA

Within the kingdom of Hungary and the neighbouring realm of Wallachia, Janos Hunyadi was the strong man between 1446 and 1456. Vlad Dracula, in his late teens and early 20s, could only try to survive in the shadow of this mighty warlord. Janos Hunyadi was the most effective military commander against the Turks in the 15th century. He won several major victories that significantly slowed the Ottoman advance in the Balkans. The legend of Hunyadi's success overwhelmed and influenced all ambitious warlords in the region, including Vlad Dracula. Hunyadi had risen from the son of a lowly Wallachian knight to governor of the kingdom of Hungary in ten years. Like his father, he achieved this recognition through martial prowess.

Hunyadi won his most important military experience against the Hussites. He absorbed their tactics and later made effective use of war wagons and firearms, even recruiting Bohemian veterans. Returning to Hungary, he was placed in command of 100 men-at-arms. Through raid and counter-raid he repelled the Turks not only from the Hungarian border but also from his homeland of Wallachia. In the winter of 1443–4, it was thought right to conduct a major offensive against the Turks. Hunyadi led an army of Hungarians, Romanians, Poles, Serbs, Bulgarians, and Bohemians. They crossed the Danube and occupied Nis and Sofia. Through speed and his skill of organisation, Hunyadi prevented the Ottoman forces from uniting and defeated them in a series of battles. By the end of the campaign, he had shattered Ottoman power in the Balkans north of Greece and won himself great fame. Sultan Murad II was forced to accept peace.

Vlad Dracul, Vlad Dracula's father, played an ambiguous role in this campaign. Vlad Dracul was a loyal and successful knight. In 1431, he was made a member of the Order of the Dragon by King Sigismund of Hungary, hence his name. Dracula simply means son of Dracul. The Order of the Dragon was dedicated to the destruction of heretics and infidels. But at the time of Hunyadi's campaign, Dracul was prince of Wallachia, enthroned by Sigismund. He had no wish to ride on a crusade against the Turks. He knew well the power of the Ottomans. Living directly on the Danube frontier of their conquests in the Balkans, he would be the first to suffer from any conflict. Since 1437, Dracul had signed an alliance with Murad II and even accompanied the Sultan on raids into Transylvania, a province of Hungary. In 1441, Hunyadi demanded that Dracul renew his pledge to the Order of the Dragon and resist the Turks. But the next year, Dracul allowed the Turks to pass through Wallachia and ravage Transylvania. Hunyadi defeated the Ottomans near Sibiu, pursued them into Wallachia and at the same time removed Dracul from his throne. Dracul sought sanctuary with the Turks and was forced into even closer agreement with the Sultan. In 1443 he was replaced on the Wallachian throne. To secure his alliance with the Turks, they demanded two of his sons as hostages: Radu and Dracula. They were held in a castle in western Anatolia in Turkey.

In the autumn of 1444, the victorious Hungarians hoped to push the remaining Turkish presence out of Europe altogether. They broke their peace treaty. An international crusader army advanced on the town of Varna on the Black Sea coast to break the Turkish ring around Constantinople. A Venetian-Burgundian fleet endeavoured to occupy the Dardancllcs to stop Ottoman reinforcements from Asia. The fleet failed, probably because of Genoese treachery, and the Sultan crossed with a mighty army to confront the Hungarians at Varna. The battle began well for Hunyadi. Bohemians, Italians, and Hungarians armed with handguns blasted the Turkish advance guard. Lightly armoured Hungarian horsemen dashed in among the Turkish warriors, shooting composite bows, throwing javelins, and slashing with their sabres. The Turks panicked. They scrambled out of the havoc. It seemed as though the Ottoman army would break. The Hungarian King and his noblemen were impatient to join the battle. They believed one final charge from their gleaming knights would have the infidels screaming back to Asia. Hunyadi urged caution. The battle was not yet won. The King ignored him. He wished to capture the Sultan, surrounded on a nearby hill by Christian janissary archers. Lances were lowered and horses spurred onwards. Several hundred knights and men-at-arms thundered towards the hill. They had miscalculated. The Turks rallied and shattered the Hungarian onslaught. The King's head was cut off by a janissary. Hunyadi narrowly escaped the slaughter.

Vlad Dracul avoided the catastrophe of Varna by sending a token force of 4,000 Wallachians under the command of his eldest son Mircea. Dracul's

Janos Hunyadi, Hungarian warlord and victorious crusader against the Turks. Woodcut published in Brno in 1488.

part involvement, however, threatened the safety of his two hostage sons. Usually, the life of a noble hostage was a comfortable one. It is likely that the boys were treated with respect, using the occasion to learn Turkish and gain an invaluable insight into Ottoman warfare. With the Hungarian declaration of war, this changed. A Turkish document records that Radu had to defend himself against the perverted sexual advances of the Sultan. He eventually succumbed, becoming a harem favourite of the Ottoman court. In this cruel, anxious atmosphere, the adolescent Dracula learned truths about fear and violence that remained with him for the rest of his life.

Following the disaster of Varna, the failed Burgundian-Venetian fleet sailed into the Black Sea and along the Danube in search of Hunyadi. According to the chronicler Jehan de Wavrin, Dracul aided the fleet with supplies and information. The eight galleys were mounted with cannon and under the command of Walerand de Wavrin, the chronicler's nephew, they assaulted several Turkish garrisons. Noting the amount of booty, Dracul appears to have had few doubts about joining the raiding campaign. On one occasion, he took personal charge of a giant bombard. Inexperienced in its use, he fired it repeatedly without allowing the barrel to cool between shots. Eventually, it burst. The bombard was repaired, but exploded again, killing a gunner. Later, Dracul proposed an ambush on the Turks under the pretence of a safe conduct. Wavrin was shocked at this deception and refused to put his seal to it. Dracul carried on regardless and the Turks were massacred.

With these minor successes behind him, Dracul was scornful of Hunyadi's defeat at Varna. When the Hungarian warlord passed through Wallachia, Dracul had him imprisoned. He laughed at Hunyadi: 'The Sultan goes hunting with more followers than were in your army.' He demanded his execution. Hunyadi's reputation saved him, but the warlord swore vengeance for this humiliation. In 1447, Hunyadi led an expedition against the prince of Wallachia. Dracul and his son Mircea were killed. Hunyadi proclaimed himself ruler of Wallachia. Later he passed the crown to Vladislav II, a loyal retainer. The Turks were angry. Dracul had been a good friend, despite occasional lapses. The next year they released Dracula. They told him to claim the throne of his dead father. Dracula emerged from captivity a bitter, determined man.

At Kosovo, Hunyadi sought revenge for Varna. He placed his German and Bohemian handgunners behind war wagons and fieldworks. He would not be dragged into rash offensives. On his flanks gathered Albanian and Wallachian horsemen, adventuring knights, and Magyar horse-archers. Vladislav II had brought 8,000 warriors and rode alongside Hunyadi. Turkish footsoldiers, still relying on crossbows and composite bows rather than firearms, dug in opposite the Christian centre. Their mail-clad horsemen waited on the wings. Neither side wished to attack first. Eventually, skirmishing broke out between the crowds of cavalry. The battle began. Gangs of horsemen charged forwards, delivered their

Armoured river-boat with cannon. Such craft were employed by the Christians against the Turks along the Danube. From the mid 15th century *Diebold Schilling Amtliche Chronik*, now in the Burgerbibliothek, Bern.

weaponry, and dashed away. Christian gunners sparked their barrels. Iron shot sunk into earth and wood. Through the smoke, crossbow bolts and arrows embedded themselves silently. Again and again the horsemen on both sides challenged each other. Wallachian nerves were strained. They snapped; the Christian centre slowly drew back. The battle lasted two days. It was hard fought. The Turks claimed a victory but gained little advantage. The true winner of Kosovo was riding hundreds of miles to the

Eques Walachus

north of the retreating Christians. With a small force of borrowed Turkish horsemen, Dracula snatched the opportunity of Vladislav's absence. He rode into Wallachia and assumed the prince's crown. As far as he was concerned, both Vladislav and Hunyadi lay dead at Kosovo.

In the dismal retreat following Kosovo, Hunyadi was imprisoned by a Serbian lord angered at the looting of his territory by the crusader army. Instead of trying to free his patron, Vladislav commandeered the remnants of the Christian army and made for Wallachia. He tracked down Dracula and defeated him. Dracula fled to the court of Moldavia, to the east of

Wallachian warrior with composite bow. Wallachians·fought in both Christian and Turkish armies.

Wallachia. In 1455, Constantinople, the bastion of Orthodox Christianity, fell to the Turks. It was a great blow to Hungary and sent a shudder through central Europe. Hunyadi feared a Turkish invasion. Dracula thought it politic to throw himself on the mercy of Hunyadi. Moldavia was too much like exile for Dracula. The court of Hunyadi was the only place for an ambitious young man. Fortunately, Hunyadi had never forgiven Vladislav for leaving him in a Serbian prison while securing his own throne. On top of this, Vladislav had succumbed to Turkish influence. The Wallachians paid a regular tribute and the new Sultan Mehmed II considered the country open

127

land across which he could attack Transylvania. Hunyadi accepted Dracula's pledges of loyalty and employed him to defend the border of Transylvania against Wallachia. It was a golden opportunity. Dracula gathered an army and awaited the time to claim back his princedom.

With typical strategic skill, Hunyadi pre-empted Turkish invasion. He rode to the relief of Belgrade, a powerful fortress controlling the southern Danube border of Hungary. Combining professional warriors with armed peasants, he battered the Turks. It was a remarkable triumph. A few days later, disease broke out among the victorious troops. Hunyadi was one of its victims. His premature death severely weakened Christian resistance in eastern Europe. But at the time, Dracula could only consider it a tremendous relief to be rid of the overwhelming presence of Hunyadi. He saw no obstacle to his ambition. He crossed the Transylvanian mountains into Wallachia. Vladislav was defeated and killed. In September 1456, Dracula became prince of Wallachia. He paid homage to both the Hungarian King and the Turkish Sultan. He already knew the reality of the situation.

Dracula made Tirgoviste in central Wallachia his capital. Within his modest palace, he plotted his initial revenge. When his father and elder brother had fled after their defeat by Hunyadi, they had received no help from the Wallachian nobility: the boyars. In Tirgoviste, Mircea had been captured by hostile boyars, tortured and then buried alive. To verify this tale, Dracula had his brother exhumed. When the earth was removed, he found Mircea face down, his body contorted. In deep silence, Dracula returned to his palace. All the principal boyars were invited to a feast. As the several hundred noblemen assembled, Dracula sent his bodyguard into the palatial hall. One by one, the boyars were dragged out and impaled on stakes outside the palace. In a dreadful night of death, the prince of Wallachia broke the power of the old nobility. The political reasoning was revealed in a question he asked the noblemen before execution. 'How many princes have ruled Wallachia in your lifetime?' None were so young that they had not known at least seven. At this Dracula grew angry. 'It is because of your intrigues and feuds that the principality is weak.' Dracula replaced the massacred boyars with a new nobility. Many warriors were elevated from their free peasant families: the *viteji*. Loyalty mattered above background. The prince surrounded himself with men committed to defending his regime. He raised a personal bodyguard from friendly boyars and mercenaries: the *sluji*.

Despite his control over the nobility, Dracula never felt completely secure. Wallachian subjects were impaled for the most trivial reasons. This method of execution, so characteristic of Dracula, earned him the Romanian nickname Tepes: 'the impaler'. He inflicted on others the misery and pain he had suffered in Turkish captivity. A German print of 1499 records Dracula dining among the dead and dying bodies of Saxon merchants captured in a raid. No execution or torture was too revolting for Dracula to witness with pleasure. The German settlers of Transylvania and especially

Dracula, prince of Wallachia, 15th century woodcut based upon a near contemporary oil painting.

the Saxon merchants of Brasov wielded great economic power. Whenever they refused Dracula's one-sided treaties, the Wallachian brutally destroyed their communities. They never forgave Dracula and relentlessly conspired against him, spreading their accounts of his atrocities to western Europe. At a time of many bloodthirsty warlords, even his contemporaries considered him excessively violent.

The close relationship between Wallachia and the Turks continued into the first years of Dracula's reign. The treaty he signed with the Turks demanded an annual tribute of 10,000 gold ducats. It also expected a constant stream of Wallachian boys for training as Ottoman janissaries. Turkish pressgangs frequently raided the country to ensure the human tribute. Dracula refused to accept this. The raiders were becoming bold and captured several castles along the Wallachian Danube border. Dracula retaliated. To bring an end to the deteriorating relationship, Mehmed II invited the prince to meet one of his representatives on the border. The governor of Nicopolis, Hamza Pasha, prepared an ambush. News of the deception reached Dracula as he approached a frontier fortress called Giurgiu. His horsemen surprised Hamza Pasha. Then, pretending to be Turks, they ordered the garrison at Giurgiu to open its gates. The Wallachians entered with the Turks and slaughtered the defenders. The

Dracula dining among the impaled bodies of his enemies. German propaganda woodcut of 1499 published in reaction to Dracula's atrocities against German settlers in Transylvania.

town was set ablaze and the Turks impaled. In respect of his rank, the tallest stake was reserved for Hamza Pasha.

Dracula continued along the Danube to the Black Sea, raiding and destroying. 'We have killed 23,884 Turks and Bulgars,' he wrote to Matthias Corvinus, new King of Hungary and son of Hunyadi. 'That's not counting all those burned in their houses and whose heads were not collected by our officials. Your majesty must be aware that I have broken the peace with the Turk not for my own sake, but for the sake of the honour of your Highness, for the defence of Christianity, and the strengthening of Catholic Law.' None of these considerations had ever been high among Dracula's priorities before, but he was desperate for military aid and hoped the magic of crusade would work. To enforce his request for help, Dracula had two bags of Turkish heads, ears, and noses sent to Buda. The King was not impressed. Dracula's other neighbours also offered only sympathy. Nevertheless, the success of Dracula's Danube campaign did cause excitement in courts further west. Could this be the rise of another Hunyadi? In 1459, Pope Pius II invited Christendom to organise a crusade against the Ottomans. Mehmed II had occupied Bosnia, Serbia, and Peloponnesian Greece. Only Albania continued to resist under the valiant guerrilla leader George Skanderberg. But every major state had its excuses. The French King could do nothing until relations with England had improved. The German Emperor could not depend on his princes. The Polish King was fighting the Teutonic Order. The Venetians asked for too much money. Dracula stood alone.

By the spring of 1462, Mehmed II raised an army some 60,000 strong to strike back at the insolent Wallachian prince. It included Balkan janissaries and Turkish soldiers from Asia Minor; 4,000 auxiliary Wallachian horsemen, among them boyar exiles, were led by Radu. The Sultan considered Dracula's submissive brother an excellent candidate for the Wallachian throne. The realisation of what faced him spurred Dracula to gather an army 30,000 in number. His boyars and their retainers were augmented by Wallachian and Bulgarian peasants. Men who distinguished themselves in battle were instantly promoted to officer rank. These *viteji* shaped the unprofessional mass into an army. The Turks advanced in two parts. The main force, led by the Sultan Mehmed, sailed along the Danube. A supporting land force marched from Philipopolis in Bulgaria. They met at the port of Vidin, one of the few Danube towns not destroyed by Dracula. As the Turks moved along the river, Dracula's horsemen kept them shadowed. When the Ottomans prepared to disembark on the northern bank, the Wallachians burst from the forest and let fly with their bows, forcing the Turks back into their boats. A few miles further on, the Turkish army finally crossed the Danube under cover of night and numerous cannons.

'A few of us first crossed the river and dug ourselves in trenches,' remembered a Serbian janissary, Constantin of Ostrovitza. 'We then set up

Mehmed II, conqueror of Constantinople and the Balkans, chief Turkish adversary of Dracula. Portrait attributed to Sinan Bey, around 1475, now in the Topkapi Palace Museum,, Istanbul.

the cannon around us. The trenches were to protect us from their horsemen. After that, we returned to the other side to transport the rest of the janissaries across. When all the footsoldiers were over, we prepared to move against the army of Dracula together with all our artillery and equipment. But as we set up the cannon, 300 janissaries were killed by the Wallachians. The Sultan could see a battle developing across the river and was saddened that he could not join us. He feared we might all be killed. However, we defended ourselves with 120 cannon and eventually repelled the Wallachian army. Then the Sultan sent over more men called *azapi* and

Dracula gave up trying to prevent the crossing and withdrew. After crossing the Danube himself, the Sultan gave us 30,000 ducats to divide among us.'

Cannon and handguns were by now a common power in eastern European armies. The development of wet-mixed gunpowder in the 15th century was a key factor in the increased efficiency of these weapons. Saltpetre was allowed to dissolve in water and percolate into charcoal. On drying, the active ingredients resided within the charcoal, rather than separately as they had before, and so produced a finer mixture which ignited immediately. When dried and squeezed through sieves to produce a powder of uniform grain size, it ensured a more consistent reaction. Recent firing tests with simulated medieval handguns revealed that a gun using 14th century dry-mixed powder misfired once in every four shots, whereas a gun using 15th century wet-mixed powder misfired one time in ten. Firing a steel bullet at steel armour, one tenth of an inch thick, a wet-mix gun penetrated five times out of eight, whereas a dry mix gun did not penetrate at all. By the middle of the 15th century, firearms were a vital element in Turkish armies in the Balkans. They gained much from the expertise of captured and bribed Christian gun-makers. The city of Dubrovnik and Venetian gun-runners were frequent suppliers of artillery to the Turks despite Christian bans on supplying arms to them.

Dracula realised the impossibility of confronting the Turks in open combat. He decided upon a guerrilla war with a scorched earth withdrawal. Crops were burned, wells poisoned, livestock and peasants absorbed within the army. The Turks were slowed down by the lack of food and the intense summer heat. It was so hot, the Turks were said to cook shish kebab on their sun-heated rings of mail. At night, the Sultan insisted on surrounding his army with earthworks. The janissary Constantin recalled the frequent raids made by Dracula's warriors. 'With a few horsemen, often at night, using hidden paths, Dracula would come out of the forest and destroy Turks too far from their camp.' The psychological strain of the guerrilla warfare began to tell. 'A terrible fear crept into our souls,' continued the janissary. 'Even though Dracula's army was small, we were constantly on guard. Every night we used to bury ourselves in our trenches. And yet we still never felt safe.' In the Carpathian mountains overlooking Tirgoviste, Dracula planned his most famous night raid. He gathered several thousand of his finest horsemen. Captured Turkish warriors were subjected to hideous torture and precise information extracted from them. Dracula wanted to capture the Sultan.

At nightfall, Dracula's forces assembled in the dim forest. Through ferns and brushwood, they trod silently. Turkish guards were stifled. Suddenly, all hell broke loose. Swinging sabres, yelping like wolves, shooting bows, the Wallachian horsemen descended on the Turkish camp. Slashing through tents and warriors slumped by fires, Dracula's warriors were everywhere. They searched for the Sultan's tent. A particularly grand structure caught their attention. They tore down the rich material, cut down its defenders, two viziers were slaughtered. But they were not the Sultan. While the majority of Turks panicked, Mehmed's janissaries picked up their arms and assembled around their master's tent. If only Dracula's other commander joined the attack, then the loyal but small force could be overcome. But the boyar had lost his nerve. The janissaries raised their bows and handguns. The majority of the Wallachians were content to massacre the more vulnerable Turks and load themselves with loot, before disappearing back into the forest. Dracula was furious. The Sultan had been within his grasp. Mehmed survived the night of slaughter, but he had lost several thousand of his men in a traumatic combat. It was the nearest the two forces would come to a major battle throughout the campaign.

Shaken but undeterred, the Turks advanced on Tirgoviste. Just outside the city, Mehmed came across a mile-long gorge. It was filled with the most terrible of sights. Over 20,000 contorted, rotting bodies, many of them Turkish, were perched on a forest of stakes: impaled on the orders of Dracula. The Sultan was revolted by the scale of the horror. Dracula had finally pierced the Sultan's brutal mind with his terror. 'Overcome by disgust,' wrote the Byzantine chronicler Chalcondylas, 'the Sultan admitted he could not win this land from a man who does such things. A man who knows how to exploit the fear of his people.' The main Turkish army was ordered to withdraw eastwards. The night attacks and the spread of disease among his soldiers were probably the main reasons for Mehmed's reluctance to assault Tirgoviste, but Dracula's terrorism should not be underestimated. Throughout Christendom, the Turkish withdrawal was received as Dracula's victory.

Before leaving Wallachia, Mehmed gave Radu permission to seize Dracula's crown. He left a small force of Turkish warriors under Radu's command. By this stage, Dracula was exhausted. His guerrilla warfare had damaged his own people as much as the Turks. Many of his loyal boyars were disappointed that Dracula had not achieved an outright victory and finished the Turkish menace completely. Radu realised that most Wallachians were desperate for a return to peace. He talked with the leading nobles. They were happy to become a tribute-paying ally of the Turks again in return for an end to hostilities. Radu built on Dracula's resistance of Mehmed to gain greater independence for his country, but chose reconciliation to secure a rapid peace. The boyars proclaimed 'a victory can sometimes be more harmful to the victorious than the defeated.'

German sallet, between 1450 and 1460. Dracula and most eastern European knights wore arms and armour derived from German models. Now in the Wallace Collection, London.

Turkish iron cannons of the 15th century. The Turks were slow to adopt firearms but gained much from their contact with Christian gun-makers in the Balkans and learned to use them to great effect. Outside the Military Museum, Istanbul.

By the end of the year, Radu had been recognised as prince of Wallachia by most boyars and the King of Hungary. The Turks were happy.

Rejected by his people and with few resources, Dracula escaped to the mountains of Transylvania. There, he licked his wounds in the fortress of Arges. Perched among the craggy Carpathian range, this was Dracula's Castle. According to local folklore, Radu pursued his brother along the valley of the Arges river. He set Turkish cannons on a hill opposite Dracula's castle and began to pound it. A final assault was prepared for the next day. During the night, a slave, a distant relative of Dracula, crept out of the Turkish camp to warn the former prince. He attached a message to an arrow and shot it through a window of the castle. Informed of their fate, Dracula's wife declared she would rather have her 'body eaten by the fish than become a Turkish slave'. She threw herself from the battlements, plummeting into the river below. Dracula decided on a less fatal escape. He slipped out of the castle, climbed the rocky slopes, and rode for Brasov, where the King of Hungary had made his headquarters during this crisis. The arrival of the ragged, exhausted, desperate Wallachian was nothing but an embarrassment to the King. Having already recognised Radu as the new prince, the King had Dracula escorted to a prison in Buda.

Dracula remained in prison for 12 years. One chronicler relates that even in his cell he inflicted pain on others. He caught mice and impaled them. But this is propaganda. In reality, Dracula resided at the Hungarian court under house arrest. King Matthias considered it useful to have a claimant to the Wallachian crown among his court. Besides, Dracula's brutal talents might be needed in another crusade against the Turks. Dracula married into the Hungarian royal family. He renounced Greek Orthodoxy to become a Roman Catholic. In Wallachia, this conversion was considered a heresy and all such heretics were said to become vampires after death. Catholicism eased Dracula's path to freedom. He was given the rank of captain in the Hungarian army. Often, King Matthias would have Dracula presented to visiting Turkish envoys to assure them he could be unleashed at any time. The Turks still feared him.

By 1475, Stephen, prince of Moldavia, was keen for an alliance with Hungary. He saw little difference between the Turks and the Wallachians and wished to secure his western and southern borders against them. He proclaimed a crusade and invited the King of Hungary to join him. King Matthias was happy to receive funds for this campaign from the Pope, but created more noise than action. By himself, Stephen moved against Radu and deposed him. Radu received Turkish help and fought back. To protect the Transylvanian border against Wallachian raids, Dracula was placed in command of frontier forces. Once in the saddle, he resumed his war of terror. A papal envoy reported that Dracula cut the Turks to pieces and impaled the bits on separate stakes. At the battle of Vashi, Stephen, with possibly Dracula in his ranks, won a great victory against the Wallachians and the Turks. The triumph was followed by a formal alliance between Stephen and Matthias. The next year, the Hungarian King declared Dracula his candidate for the throne of Wallachia.

In the autumn of 1476, an army of 25,000 Hungarians, Transylvanians, Wallachians, and Serbs assembled in southern Transylvania. Ultimate command lay with Stephen Bathory, a loyal retainer to King Matthias, but the object was to replace Dracula on the throne of Wallachia. At the same time, a force of 15,000 Moldavians prepared to invade eastern Wallachia under Stephen. In November, Dracula descended from the snow covered Carpathians and besieged Tirgoviste. Before the massive army, the Wallachian citizens could do little. It fell without much struggle. The army moved southwards. With the capture of Bucharest, Dracula became prince of Wallachia again. The boyars were seemingly behind him. But the apparent submission of Wallachia to the old tyrant was just that. Within a couple of months, a mutilated, headless body was discovered in marshes near the monastery of Snagrov. The corpse was Dracula. The boyars could not forget the horror of his reign. With a small bodyguard of Moldavians, Dracula was surprised in a skirmish outside Bucharest. Whether it was Wallachians or Turks who delivered the final blows is unknown. Indeed, the exact circumstances of the assassination remain a mystery. What is certain is that Dracula's head was cut off and sent to the Sultan at Constantinople. The Turks rejoiced.

The death of Vlad Dracula did little to improve the state of Wallachia. It most certainly weakened its anti-Ottoman stance. Princes came and went and Wallachia depended increasingly on the energetic Stephen of Moldavia to preserve the Danube frontier against the Turks. In the next century, the battle was lost and the Turks surged across the river to Hungary. To the Romanians, Vlad Dracula has remained a national hero, a staunch defender of Christianity against the Turks. In western Europe, his image has undergone a devilish transformation, from triumphant crusader to bloodthirsty vampire. The latter is a creation of the 19th century imagination, consolidated in books and films. But by the late 15th century, western writers had already forgotten Dracula's crusading triumphs and repeated only horrific accounts of his cruelty. German woodcut pamphlets were the principal agents of this image, showing Dracula dining among impaled victims. The Saxon merchants of Transylvania and their German neighbours never forgave Dracula for his raids and crimes against their people. Through their history they forever damned Dracula as the cruellest of medieval warlords.

BIBLIOGRAPHY

This is, of necessity, a select bibliography of both primary and secondary sources.

AETIUS:

Flavius Merobaudes, *Panegyrics I & II*. Courtly praise by a contemporary. Translation and commentary by F. M. Clover, Transactions of the American Philosophical Society, vol. 61 pt. 1, pp. 3–78, Philadelphia, 1971.

Renatus Frigeridus, brief biography of Aetius preserved in Gregory of Tour's *History of the Franks*. Translated by L. Thorpe, London, 1974.

Sidonius Apollinaris, *Panegyrics*. References to Aetius and his followers written later in the 5th century. Translated by W. B. Anderson, London, 1936.

Jordanes, *Gothic History*. The most detailed account of the war between Aetius and Attila, 6th century. Translated by C. C. Mierow, Princeton, 1915.

John of Antioch and Priscus. Fragments collected and translated by C. D. Gordon, *The Age of Attila*, Michigan, 1960.

Freeman, E. A., 'Aetius and Boniface', *The English Historical Review*, vol. 2, no. 7, pp. 417–465, London, 1887.

Maenchen-Helfen, J. O., *The World of the Huns*, Los Angeles, 1973.

Thompson, E. A., *Romans and Barbarians*, Wisconsin, 1982.

GAISERIC:

Saint Augustine, letters to Boniface. Translated by M. Dods, Edinburgh, 1875.

Possidius, *Life of St Augustine*. By a contemporary who experienced the seige of Hippo. Translated by F. R. Hoare, London, 1954.

Procopius, *History of the Vandal Wars*. By a 6th century Byzantine. Translated by H. B. Dewing, London, 1916.

Hydatius, *Chronicles*. A 5th century account of Spanish history. French translation by A. Tranoy, Paris, 1974.

Curtois, C., *Les Vandales et l'Afrique*, Paris, 1955.

Casson, L., *Ships and Seamanship in the Ancient World*, Princeton, 1971.

AN LU-SHAN:

Levy, H. S., *Biography of An Lu-shan*. Extracts from the Chiu T'ang-shu. Translated and annotated, Berkeley, 1960.

Pulleyblank, E. G., *The Background of the Rebellion of An Lu-shan*, Oxford, 1955.

Pulleyblank, E. G., 'The An Lu-shan rebellion and the origins of chronic militarism in late T'ang China', *Essays on T'ang Society*, edited by J. C. Perry & B. L. Smith, Leiden, 1976.

des Rotours, R., *Histoire de Ngan Lou-chan*, Paris, 1962.

Twitchett, D. (editor), *The Cambridge History of China*, vol. 3 pt. 1, Cambridge, 1979.

Kwanten, L., *Imperial Nomads*, Leicester, 1979.

OWEN OF WALES:

Jean Froissart, *Chronicles*. Written towards the end of the 14th century and gathered from first-hand witnesses. Several translations.

Davies, J. H., 'Owen Lawgoch-Yevain de Galles', *Montgomeryshire Collections*, vol. 37, pp. 233–256, Oswestry, 1915.

Owen, E., 'Yevain de Galles: some facts and suggestions', *Montgomeryshire Collections*, vol. 36, pp. 144–216, Oswestry, 1912.

Rhys, Professor, 'Welsh Cave Legends and the story of Owen Lawgoch', *Montgomeryshire Collections*, vol. 36, pp. 141–144, Oswestry, 1912.

Anderson, R. C., *Oared Fighting Ships*, London, 1962.

Anderson, R. C., *The Sailing Ship*, London, 1926.

GUESCLIN:

Jean Cuvelier, *Chronique de Bertrand du Guesclin*. Epic poem written about 1380. Edited by E. Charriere, Paris, 1839.

Jean Froissart, *Chronicles*. As above.

Dupuy, M., *Bertrand du Guesclin, Capitaine d'Aventure, Connétable de France*, Paris, 1978.

Thompson, H. Y., *Illustrations from the Life of Guesclin by Cuvelier*, from a manuscript of about 1400, London, 1909.

Vercel, R., *Bertrand of Brittany*, translated by M. Saunders, London, 1934.

ZIZKA:

Aeneas Sylvius, *Historia Bohemica*. Fullest 15th century account of Zizka's life. Several editions, no translation.

Heymann, F. G., *John Zizka and the Hussite Revolution*, Princeton, 1955.

Kaminsky, H., *A History of the Hussite Revolution*, Berkeley, 1967.

Macek, J., *The Hussite Movement in Bohemia*, Prague, 1958.

Wagner, E., *Medieval Costume, Armour and Weapons 1350–1450*, London, 1958.

Joannes Dlugosz, *Historia Polonica*. Fullest 15th century account of the battle of Tannenberg. Several editions, no translation.

Evans, G., *Tannenberg 1410:1914*, London, 1970.

DRACULA:

Florescu, R., & McNally, R. T., *Dracula*, London, 1973.

Stoicescu, N., *Vlad Tepes*, Bucharest, 1978.

Lajos, E., *Hunyadi*, Budapest, 1952.

Petrovic, D., 'Firearms in the Balkans on the eve of and after the Ottoman Conquests of the 14th and 15th centuries', *War, Technology and Society in the Middle East*, London, 1975.

Williams, A. R., 'Some Firing Tests with Simulated 15th century Handguns', *Journal of the Arms and Armour Society*, vol. 8, pp. 114–120, London, 1974.

ACKNOWLEDGEMENTS

All colour illustrations by Angus McBride Illustrations on pages 15, 20, 41, 44, 45, 46, 50, 53, 54, 56, 57, 58, 61, 62 and 74 courtesy of the British Museum, London; all other pictures courtesy of Peter Newark's Historical Pictures, Bath.

140

INDEX

144